LEVEL UP

LEVEL UP

HOW TO GET FOCUSED,
STOP PROCRASTINATING,
AND UPGRADE
YOUR LIFE

ROB DIAL

HarperOne
An Imprint of HarperCollinsPublishers

HarperCollins books may be purchased for educational, business, or sales promotional use. For information, please email the Special Markets Department at SPsales@harpercollins.com.

FIRST EDITION

Designed by Leah Carlson-Stanisic

Library of Congress Cataloging-in-Publication Data has been applied for.

ISBN 978-0-06-322470-4

23 24 25 26 27 LBC 5 4 3 2 1

Dedicated to my mom. Thank you for always encouraging me to follow my heart and never give up, no matter how hard life gets. And more than anything else, thank you for being my hero.

Contents

LEVEL UP

Introduction

Are you your own worst enemy?

Most people say they have goals. Some want more money, others a better job, while some seek more happiness in their relationships. Despite those good intentions and people's best efforts to make choices that will improve their lives, their biggest obstacle remains themselves. They want to get better, they want to take things to the next level, yet few people achieve the success and happiness they desire simply because they can't get out of their own way, and they don't understand why.

When I was twenty-four, this was exactly my problem. I was a top-performing sales rep and had transitioned into what I thought was a dream job leading a new field office. I did what I thought I was supposed to do—dive into work and make money. And for a little while, things were going well. I was making very good money, but after working 110 hours a week for a couple of years straight, I burned out and hit rock bottom. By October 2010, I had lost all the money I had put into the company I was trying to build. And although I watched it all happen in real time, I felt powerless to change my behavior.

I did a lot of soul searching and realized that underneath my behavior was the fear of not being *enough.* This limiting belief was rooted in my past. I grew up with an alcoholic father whose disease caused him to put me in dangerous situations on more than one occasion. Even when I wasn't in immediate danger, I always felt like I came second in his life, after alcohol. He died when I was fifteen, and it took me years to realize the emotional toll his alcoholism had taken on me. Only later did I understand that I was trying to succeed not for myself, but so that I could finally prove that I was worthy of the love that I never felt from him. If I was ever going to achieve my version of success or happiness, I needed to get in touch with my passion, and better understand what I wanted out of life.

There was one part of my sales job that I loved, and that was being able to make an impact on the younger employees I trained. That's what gave me the most fulfillment. I knew that I was an excellent listener. I had wanted to be a psychologist for a long time, and the parts of my job that I enjoyed the most were the parts that resembled being a psychologist. I may have lost the money I had earned, but nobody could take away the knowledge I had built up over the years. I realized that I could tell people my story, and maybe they could find inspiration in it and do the same.

That was the birth of my podcast, *The Mindset Mentor.* I didn't know what I was doing or whether this whole experiment would work, but I didn't care. I didn't worry about going viral or how to monetize any of my content. I focused only on trying to help people by talking about all of the different things that helped me. I treated it like a diary at first. I would say what I needed to say to myself. I was an open book. No subject was off-limits, and I was as vulnerable as possible. I had learned that healing was only possible when letting those emotions go. It wasn't easy at first, and I made mistakes, but I didn't give up. I stuck with it, adjusted, and got better. I've since gone on to record more than thirteen hundred podcasts and have over two hundred million podcast downloads.

Today, I run two companies: a school that helps business owners grow and scale their businesses, and the Mindset Mentor, which includes my podcast and self-development classes. My clients and listeners are all looking for wisdom, tools, and strategies that will help them find success in the most important areas of their lives: business, relationships, health, money, family, and more.

After coaching thousands of people, I've learned that most of them know exactly what they need to do to achieve their goals and become successful. Whether they want to lose weight, make more money, or have better relationships, figuring out *what* they need to do isn't the problem. That information is out there and readily available, but they aren't doing it. Why? It's because they don't know *how* to take the action required to get started. Taking action is not what causes problems; it's what fixes them. I don't know anyone who has more problems because they took the action required to get the life they want. The harsh reality is that you cannot change your life unless you commit to deciding what that first step is and taking it.

This book is for those people who know they have potential but aren't realizing that potential or making the impact they know they can make on the world. This is a book for those who have tried multiple times to get going, and probably made some excellent progress right out of the gate but suddenly found themselves struggling to drum up the motivation to keep at it. The diet and exercise routine didn't stick, or maybe that business plan never materialized. After feeling so good at first, they got derailed, discouraged, and were left thinking it was impossible to get what they wanted.

The problem is that most people are looking for that one key that will unlock success, but it doesn't exist. There is no magic word that will make all your dreams come true. Success is not one big event that changes your life. Success comes from the accumulation of many small actions—what I call *micro-actions*—that you take every single day. The state of your relationships, the amount of money you have in the bank, and your career trajectory are all a result of the micro-actions you took in the past. That means your future will be determined by the micro-actions you take from here on out. It's not about being the best; it's about being better than you were yesterday. You can't compare yourself to other people. When you go to bed at night, the only thing that matters is that you improved that day. It's about showing up for yourself through the action you take today.

> Success comes from the accumulation of many small actions—what I call *micro-actions*—that you take every single day.

Fortunately, yesterday is over, and you have a choice between things being hard now and easy later or easy now and hard later. Pick one, because nobody gets through life without some bumps, bruises, and a few scars. Doing hard things can be painful, both physically and emotionally, but guess what? That's good because your pain is a stimulus for growth. When you go to the gym, you need to break down your muscles so they can grow back stronger; your brain works the same way. You need to push through that discomfort and get out of your comfort zone to grow and change. The trick is not giving yourself a choice.

In *The Art of War*, Sun Tzu wrote about the need for armies to burn their boats and bridges after arriving on enemy shores because soldiers without the option of retreat are more likely to fight to victory. This was a technique used by Alexander the Great, Spanish captain Hernán Cortés, and several other military leaders who recognized the importance of going all in. You want to do the same. Fully commit!

Once you're on board, this process begins by identifying why you haven't been taking action and then clearing the runway. Once you learn what's holding you back, you can then remove the obstacles standing in your way to begin implementing the tiny micro-actions, rituals, and habits that will get you moving in the direction you want to go. It's important also to understand the science of the brain. What's incredible is that as you lean into taking action, your brain actually starts to change. The brain has the ability to adapt by forming and reorganizing synaptic connections, called *neuroplasticity*, and with the work you put in on the front end, these new connections in your brain will make taking consistent action easier, so this change will stick.

I've found taking action comes down to six steps, and if you follow these six steps when pursuing a goal, you *will* see results. The six steps are:

1. Focus

2. Work

3. Persist

4. Rest

5. Reward

6. Repeat

We'll go through each step together in the following chapters, and review them in the epilogue.

Through trial and error, I've learned what works and what doesn't, but this isn't a book about only me and I don't rely only on anecdotal evidence. It tells the story of the clients I've coached through the same issues you're experiencing right now. The most common challenges are related to diet, fitness, money, business, and relationships, so those are primary examples I provide, but this same approach can work no matter what the challenge you're trying to overcome or the goal you hope to achieve. In addition to strategies and tips on how to incorporate these concepts into your daily life, I cite the science that supports what I've learned from the experts I've interviewed on my podcast. This process requires a mindset shift, and a better understanding of how your brain works makes the shift much easier—but that's a complicated subject. As author and speaker Tony Robbins once said on my podcast, "Complexity is the enemy of execution," so I've set out to make this information as simple and straightforward as possible. I've also included journal prompts at the end of each chapter. These will help you better understand the process and push you forward, while also helping you see how much you've already changed. For more journal prompts and video lessons from this book, go to RobDial.com/LevelUp.

Life is pretty simple: either you achieve your goals or you don't. The difference almost always comes down to whether you take the action necessary to get what you want. That's the missing link for so many people, but this book provides a simple step-by-step blueprint to help you take the action required every single day, so that you can create the life that you want. That is how you level up. And you don't have to wait. This is a process you will begin immediately. Let's go get things done!

> Life is pretty simple: either you achieve your goals or you don't.

Part I

WHY YOU'RE NOT TAKING ACTION

This book is filled with strategies to help you create the life you want, but none of that matters if you can't get past what is holding you back from taking action in the first place. In Part I, we take a look under the hood of the car to understand why, despite your best efforts and strongest wishes, you haven't been taking action, or in some cases, sustaining the action long enough. The answer boils down to three main reasons: fear, the story you're telling yourself, and the lack of a clear purpose.

The first step is understanding the nature of fear and how most of what you're scared of isn't real, which we'll explore in Chapter 1. You say that you want to do something but then immediately persuade yourself that you can't do it. You might be scared of failure or not being good enough. You might be scared of what people think. Ultimately, you're scared of a future that hasn't happened yet, so you do what's safe. Nothing. You take yourself out of the race before you even start. Once you learn that those fears aren't real, you can take that first step outside of your comfort zone, which is where true change occurs.

The second step is confronting the story that is constantly running in the back of your mind, and this is where we'll go in Chapter 2. You probably don't even know the story is there most of the time. Everything you've experienced over the years has been stored in your brain, forming a story about who you believe you are. You have become a character. That character is your identity, and it's very convincing in telling you what you can and can't do. The good news is that character is a story you made up. It's not real, so you can change it. And I will teach you how to change your story, so it will no longer hold you back.

Once you can properly identify fear for what it is and change the story you're telling yourself, you must define exactly what it is you want, which we'll explore in Chapter 3. Like most people, I'm sure you have a vague idea. You might want to lose weight or make more money, but what does that mean? You can't hit a target you can't see, so get specific. When your goals are crystal clear, you will feel pulled toward the future you want, and visualization, which we will discuss in Chapter 4, can help accelerate that process. When you reach that point, you will be primed and ready to take action, but let's start at the beginning. What are you scared of?

CHAPTER 1

Fear

None of It Is Real

I am terrified of spiders, and I can link that fear back to my sister.

The movie *Arachnophobia* was a horror-comedy that came out in 1990. Starring John Goodman and Jeff Daniels, it was about a small town that was invaded by a rare and very dangerous species of spider. When I was five, my older sister described scenes from the movie in such vivid detail that it scared the absolute hell out of me. Two scenes in particular stand out. The first was when a spider caught fire and chased after someone. I can't think of anything that sounds scarier than that, except for maybe the second scene she described, where a spider crawled into the toilet right before one of the characters entered the bathroom and sat on the toilet without looking inside first. For the next three years, I made sure to thoroughly check the toilet before I sat down. I'm still terrified of spiders, but how is this possible?

My fear of spiders is not my fear. It didn't even come from the movie because I never watched it. I learned this fear from my sister. And if a fear that fierce could be built into me by another person, how many other fears have I picked up over the years from friends, family, and society in general? The answer is probably most of them! The thing is, fear is natural; it tells us when we might need to pay attention and be cautious about something. But not all fears are equal, so how do we know which fears are worth paying attention to?

Which Fears Are Real, and Which Are Imagined?

I turned to psychologists, gurus, and neurobiologists, and after going into every nook and cranny to study fear, I was surprised to learn that human beings are born with only two fears:

1. **The fear of falling.**

2. **The fear of loud noises.**

These are the only fears that are built into our brain circuitry, and they emerge as soon as we are born.

In 1960, Eleanor J. Gibson and Richard D. Walk at Cornell University conducted the "visual cliff" experiment with infants between six and fourteen months old.[1] They discovered that even when the children were called by their mothers, almost all of the infants would not crawl out over a heavy glass that was designed to look like a cliff. Instinctually, even babies were scared of falling. Meanwhile, the fear of loud noises, or what has become known as the "acoustic startle response," is a defense mechanism or a warning of potential danger designed to keep us safe.[2] These two fears are innate to almost all humans, regardless of the culture we were born into; but how do we know that fear is a behavior that can be so easily learned?

In 1919, John B. Watson and Rosalie Rayner at Johns Hopkins University conducted what became known as the Little Albert Experiment. Nine-month-old Albert was exposed to numerous objects and animals, including a white rat, to which he exhibited no fear. Two months later, the researchers isolated Albert with only the rat, and every time he went to touch the rat, they struck a steel bar with a hammer, creating a loud noise that startled Albert and caused him to cry. They did this repeatedly, and eventually Albert became distressed and fearful at the mere sight of the rat. He went from having no fear of the rat to being terrified of the rat. It's no surprise that this experiment has since been criticized for being unethical, but it opened the door to further research on how fears can be learned.

If the fear of falling and the fear of loud noises are the only two innate fears that we're born with, this means that every single other fear is learned. They come from our environment, and we pick them up by watching and listening to our friends, family, and what's happening around us in our society. If your parents are afraid of people judging them, there is a good chance you might have that same fear, too.

I've spent a lot of time discussing fear with my clients and how it can prevent them from taking action. Over time, I saw patterns develop and realized that people's inability to take action could be traced back to the same five fears. Almost every fear is a version of one of these fears.

1. FEAR OF FAILURE: This is the fear that you won't reach your goals. It can lead to your being indecisive and procrastinating. You might even tell people you're going to fail just to keep expectations low. The fear of failure is also referred to as atychiphobia.

2. FEAR OF REJECTION: This is a fear of people telling you "no" or turning you down. It can be personal (like a relationship) or professional (with your business). It's a fear of other people's opinions and judgment. Social anxiety can fall into this category.

3. FEAR OF SUCCESS: This is a fear of getting what you want. It's often rooted in the fear of change and can lead to self-sabotage. Fear of success has also been referred to as backlash avoidance, and it can alienate you from those you care about most.

4. FEAR OF BEING A FRAUD (imposter syndrome): This is the fear of being exposed as a fraud, or the fear that you aren't good enough.

5. FEAR OF ABANDONMENT: This is a fear of being left all alone, or that you might do or say something to drive away those you care the most about. This fear is often referred to as autophobia.

Each of these fears comes down to one thought: "I am not enough, and because I am not enough, I will never be loved."

If you are afraid of being too busy, notice how you're actually afraid that you're not capable enough to handle it all. Or maybe you're worried that you're going to negatively influence your children, which is really a fear of not being a good enough parent. Maybe it's the thought of running out of money that keeps you up at night—which is rooted in a fear that you aren't good enough to provide for yourself or your family. The list goes on. We want to fit in and be accepted. We want to feel loved, and ultimately these fears boil down to our not feeling like we are good enough to be loved.

What is your biggest fear that holds you back from taking action? To answer that, you must first understand what fear is.

The Two Types of Fear

At its core, fear is a defense mechanism. It derives from the amygdala, which is the fear-processing region of the brain. Two million years ago, the actions of the amygdala kept our species alive by helping us fear things that might happen in the future, such as being killed by a wild animal, so that we could avoid dangerous situations.

While our environment has changed over the past two million years, our brain hasn't changed much at all. Have you ever been sitting around on a beautiful day, drinking your coffee and feeling that life is good, when, out of nowhere, you're hit with a pang of fear? The reason is because things are going so well that the brain creates something to be afraid of to keep you protected. Really. That's what it does. The amygdala has nothing to do, so it creates fears when no actual danger exists. It's doing what it was designed to do, but today that holds us back from getting what we truly want. Once we become aware of this, we can work to get past those fears. It starts by learning that all fears can be broken down into two categories: primal fears and intellectual fears.

> Fear is a defense mechanism.

Primal fears are attached to the expectation of future physical pain or death. These fears aren't as common for us today, but every so often we do experience them. If you've ever gone camping and had to venture outside the safety of the campsite in the middle of the night to go to the bathroom, that flood of anxiety you may feel is a primal fear. It's warning you of potential danger (bears!) to keep you alive, but in our everyday lives, death isn't lurking around every corner as it once was. We have food, clothing, shelter, and people who care about us. In my house, I'm safe from the elements and can survive for a very long time. Even when we aren't in physical danger, the amygdala will still try to do its job, which is how we develop the second type of fear.

Intellectual fears are not related to the fears of physical pain or death, but our amygdala continues to see predators everywhere. Instead of lions, crocodiles, and bears, however, "predators" derive from the list we discussed above: the fears of failure, rejection, success, being seen as a fraud, and abandonment. We worry about whether we're good enough, smart enough, or attractive enough. We worry about what people will think of us and whether they will say "no" to what we ask of them. We worry about whether we're likable or whether we're going to fit in—but none of these fears is linked to physical pain or death. What real danger is there in rejection? You will not die from any of these things, but it doesn't matter if it's rejection or survival, our brains and bodies react the same way to intellectual fears as they do to primal fears.

These two types of fear can cause the same feeling inside your body. Primal fears are serving a function and are rational, while intellectual fears are neither, but the amygdala doesn't know the difference. It's as if we're walking through life and toward our goals wearing a foggy pair of glasses, and that fog is the fear preventing us from seeing things clearly.

A brain left to its own devices will almost always go negative. And since the brain can't tell the difference between primal and intellectual fears, that responsibility falls to you. Becoming more aware of fears is like building a muscle: the more you work it, the better you will get at rooting out those fears. You do that by identifying where fears come from, admitting that they aren't yours, and releasing them. But there is one trick that can help change your perspective.

Don't Try to Get Rid of Your Fear— Learn to Embrace It

It doesn't surprise me that one of the most common questions my clients ask me is, "How do I get rid of my fear?" I get it. Who doesn't want to learn how to overcome their fears? But the answer is, You can't overcome something that doesn't exist. That's right. Every single one of your fears isn't real! Don't believe me? Look over that list of common fears and consider your own. Are any of those fears coming to fruition in this moment? No!

Author and consultant Karl Albrecht defined fear as "an anxious feeling, caused by our anticipation of some imagined event or experience."[3] The key word in that definition is "imagined." That feeling of fear is a biological reaction to what we're *thinking*, not what's *happening*. We are making up a future in our mind that does not exist, and that future is almost always negative. It's a way that we protect ourselves. Will your new business fail in the future? It's true that not every business is successful, and even those that are often have setbacks; but the point is to focus on the present, not an imagined future. Your new business has not failed today, so there is nothing to be afraid of right now.

Many people are scared of success—even ambitious people who want to succeed. One of my clients grew up in a small, religious, middle-class town. Most of the people he knew were teachers and farmers who didn't make more than $60,000 a year. As he grew older, he feared that if he became too successful and made too much money, people in that community would view him differently and he would no longer be accepted. It's a fear of not fitting in, which is another version of the fear of abandonment.

This fear is common, because as tribal beings, none of us wants to feel lonely. We want to fit in and be accepted. Getting kicked out of the tribe once meant certain death, so it's natural to think that if we grow out of where we came from, we won't be accepted, and people will see us as an enemy. I can say with certainty that I've never known anyone who has become a successful millionaire to turn around and say, "Now all of my friends hate me."

Cornell University published a study showing that 85 percent of what we worry about never happens. And of those 15 percent of worries that do occur, 79 percent of the participants handled what occurred better than they expected. Some even learned a lesson. Do the math: 97 percent of our worries never materialize.[4] In other words, our worries are baseless and derive from our unfounded pessimistic perception. So, why are we using our mental energy worrying about nothing when we could use it to take action and be productive?

> Do the math: 97 percent of our
> worries never materialize.

As human beings, we have such complex and beautiful imaginations, but if we are not in control of those imaginations, they can get out of hand and create so many fears within us. We can control these fears, however, once we realize that almost all of them are as real as the bogeyman. We're masters of creating monsters in the form of fake circumstances and stories that *could* occur in our future. We then become terrified of that future even though it doesn't exist. How crazy is that?

If you are a worrier, or someone who focuses on the negative, don't get stuck here. My goal is to help you develop strategies to harness your mental energy so you can do the things you want to do, without fear holding you back. One trick is to turn fear on its head and use it to your advantage.

One of my first mentors taught me that very little in life is worse than the pain of regret and the feeling of getting to the end of your life and realizing that you wasted time. That stuck with me, so after watching my father die from alcoholism, I didn't worry about failure, abandonment, or not being good enough. Instead, I developed a fear of getting to the end of my life and realizing that there wasn't any more time, or that I had wasted my potential. That fear has motivated me to take action. You can do the same thing: Adopt the fear of getting to the end of your life and wishing you had done more. This fear will propel you toward the future you want. Fear is powerful, so embrace it and find a way to use it to your advantage.

What Future Pain Are You Trying to Avoid?

When studying this topic, I had an aha moment and had to turn off the music and all the other distractions in the room. **I realized that fear arises from an image in our brain of future pain.** With a primal fear, that pain is physical pain or death; with an intellectual fear, that pain is emotional pain. This is super important: every fear is about the brain trying to avoid future pain. What is the future pain that your fear is trying to get you to avoid?

> Fear arises from an image in our brain of future pain. Every fear is about the brain trying to avoid future pain.

For many people, this fear of future pain is the source of procrastination. When I ask my clients why they aren't taking action, many of them say, "I'm procrastinating." Yes, that might be true, but what they don't realize is that procrastination is a symptom and not the cause when it comes to their inability to take action. The cause is their trying to avoid a fear by running away from it. Many people who put off building their business, implementing a workout routine, or taking the action required to accomplish their goals do so because they are unconsciously (or sometimes even consciously) scared of failing.

What makes these fears debilitating is that they can prevent you from taking action. Intellectual fears change the way you feel, and how you feel is important because if you don't feel good, it's more difficult to take action. If you're not taking the action necessary to start or grow your business because you're scared of failing, that fear is holding you back. You're creating the feeling of having a failed business even though the business has not failed. If you're imagining pain in the future, why bother taking action at all? So, you avoid action to avoid the pain.

Tens of thousands of years ago when humans lived in caves, this fear was a defense mechanism that helped keep us alive. If we knew that we could get killed by a wild animal if we ventured outside the cave in the middle of the night, then maybe we decided to stay in the cave until the sun was up. It served a very important purpose back then, but does it serve us today when we're trying to live up to our potential? Absolutely not because that unwanted future becomes the source of negative energy. It's what prevents us from taking action because who wants to work toward a future that sucks?

What most people never learn is that life doesn't have to be like this. Life is too short to spend it scared, angry, anxious, sad, worried, or bogged down with negative emotions, but people act as if their brains are like a piece of concrete. They've absorbed certain fears or ideas about themselves and believe that if they've been that way all of their lives, they will be that way forever. But that's not true. You can control your brain and overcome the way it naturally defaults to the negative. That's what I'm going to teach you how to do in Part III.

> Life is too short to spend it scared,
> angry, anxious, sad, worried, or bogged
> down with negative emotions.

I know this sounds simple, but dealing with it isn't easy. I always say that you can't read the label when you're in the jar. In other words, when we're in our heads, it's difficult to understand why we feel the way we feel and why we act the way we act. We must get out of our heads for a moment to see ourselves as if we're a different person and try to work out why that person feels the way they do. Why is that person not taking action? What is that person afraid of? It's so easy to fool ourselves and give in to those intellectual fears because they feel so real. It can be overwhelming and even crippling, but it's our job to identify that fear for what it is. It's not real! Do you want an imagined fear to prevent you from taking the action necessary to get the future you want?

It's your job to make the distinction between real and imagined fear at all costs. You must learn how to become extremely self-aware of what you're feeling. The closer you look, the more you'll start to realize that you spend far too much time thinking about what you don't want, and not nearly enough time thinking about what you do want. But believe it or not, you have the choice. It's like saying, "I can choose to think about all the amazing things that could happen in the future, or I can choose to think about how I'm not worth it and send myself into a mini-depression. You know what? Mini-depression sounds good! I'm going to go with that one again." It sounds funny to say it like that, but how often do you choose to think about a negative future?

Every thought produces a chemical reaction in your brain that creates a feeling or emotion. We've all experienced this. Whenever you have a sexual thought, for instance, that creates a very specific feeling in your body. If your brain is going to imagine your future, and your body is going to feel whatever you think, why not make a conscious choice to think about a future that doesn't suck? Picture an awesome future in which you're inspired and successful. Think of how amazing your children will be instead of fearing that you're messing them up. Instead of thinking about all the ways your new business might not succeed, put that energy and focus into what needs to be done for you to be successful. Better yet, think about what it will feel like when you get there.

Try thinking of this another way. Let's say that you really have to go to the bathroom, but I tell you that a lion is in the tub. You won't want to take the action necessary to go to the bathroom. You're safe where you are, and you know it's not safe in the bathroom, so you will do whatever is necessary to avoid going into the bathroom as long as you know that lion is in there. The same thing happens if you're imagining a future that sucks. You're fearing all the things that could go wrong, and because the brain doesn't know the difference between primal and intellectual fears, you're feeling those feelings of that fake future, so of course you don't want to work toward that future because it sucks. Now, if I told you that outside your door right now is a pizza, a glass of wine, a puppy, or whatever you love and makes you happy, you would race out that door to get it, right? The same thing happens when thinking about a positive future. We'll dive more deeply into this concept in Chapter 4, but notice the difference.

Your brain will produce the chemicals necessary to trick your body into believing that future success is happening the same way it will produce the chemicals that make you feel those intellectual fears are happening right now. Thoughts create feelings, and how you feel will make it either easier or harder to take action. Taking action will be difficult at first, but you have to practice because the more you do it, the easier it gets. And with fewer fears holding you back, the easier it will be to take action. The more you try to fight it, the more you welcome what it is you fear.

Fear is designed to help you avoid future pain, but it causes you to imagine pain in your future, which prevents you from taking action. This becomes a self-fulfilling prophecy, because if you don't take action, future pain is inevitable. I'm not trying to scare you; I'm trying to be honest with you. Everything comes at a cost. Eventually, the result of not taking action will catch up to you—whether it's not living up to your potential, not following your heart, not giving your children the opportunities you want for them, or lying in your death bed and realizing that you wasted your life. By the time you realize what's happened, it might be too late.

> Eventually, the result of not taking
> action will catch up to you.

The only thing you can do to avoid pain is take action now toward the future you want. Will it be hard? Yes. Will you struggle? Yes. Will you mess up? Yes. But it will be worth it.

The Advantage of Fear

Fear serves a very specific function that we can all use to our advantage. As we've seen, fear is a physical manifestation in our bodies that keeps us inside our comfort zones in a (mostly) misguided attempt to keep us safe. But there is no worse place you can be when you want to take action because you can't grow when you're stuck in your comfort zone. Once you become aware of this, you can start pushing yourself a little bit at a time to get outside of your comfort zone. *That* is how you grow. The actor Will Smith said, "God placed the best things in life on the other side of fear." The life that you truly want, and the person that you know you can be, is on the other side of fear.

The one thing you can't afford to do is wait for fear to go away before you act because that's never going to happen. When I interviewed legendary mixed martial artist Georges St-Pierre on my podcast, he told me he felt terrified leading up to every one of his fights. That fear didn't go away until he stepped into the octagon. If he had ever given in to that fear, he never would have participated in a single fight; but because he fought through that instinct and stepped beyond his comfort zone, he became an icon of the sport.

True growth comes from feeling fear and deciding to do the thing you are afraid of anyway. A study published in 2018 conducted by researchers at Yale University found that growth occurs only with uncertainty.[5] The brain has no reason to learn when things are predictable and stable. You don't need to wait until you believe in yourself or for the fear to disappear before you take action. You just have to lean into that fear because that is the only way you're going to take the action necessary to change your brain and your life. You can't open the parachute before you jump off the ledge. You must jump knowing that the parachute will open.

It's not going to be easy. Your brain doesn't like change. It will always take the path of least resistance, so it's going to fight you and try to do everything to persuade you to get back in your comfort zone. Sometimes it will be with small things (hit the snooze button and go back to sleep), and sometimes it will be with much bigger and more important life decisions (don't bother starting your own business because you aren't good enough and it will fail anyway). Either way, you can't negotiate your way out of it. The only way to overcome that fear is through action, which requires consistent effort on your part.

Listen, I'll start with the bad news first: there is no hack or quick fix that will allow you to suddenly rewire your brain; it's a process, and one that we will cover in detail in Part III. But there is good news: a process is made up of steps, and we are all capable of taking a single step. I will break down the steps into the micro-actions that you can take to get real results. Creating that change will require focus and a lot of repetition, but it will happen as long as you don't allow fear to prevent you from taking that first step.

Your fears, and that voice inside your head, are showing you exactly what you need to overcome to create the life you want. Every time you feel fear and your instinct is to step back, you must lean forward instead. You don't have to steamroll ahead, but if you can make a habit of pushing yourself a little bit out of your comfort zone every time you feel fear, you will build your resilience against your fears. Fear is letting you know that you have reached the edge of your comfort zone. It's a sign of what you need to push past so you can grow. If you do that enough, years from now your comfort zone will be much larger. And one day, you won't think twice about doing things that might terrify you today. One of my first mentors used to say, "The mind is like a plastic bag: once it expands, it will never return to its original size." Your comfort zone is the same way, but you must put in the work.

> Fear is letting you know that you have reached the edge of your comfort zone. It's a sign of what you need to push past so you can grow.

You've already been doing this your entire life. It started when you were a baby learning to walk. At first, you struggled to take a single step. But soon, you were running, and then you were climbing structures at the playground. As you grew older, you might have been scared of trying out for a sport, taking a class, asking someone out on a date, but once you did it, the fear disappeared, and you grew as a person. We can all think of things that felt daunting at first, but once we did them, we could look back in amazement at how far we had come.

You will do things that others find challenging, simply because you expanded your comfort zone. That is how you set yourself apart from everyone else. If this is important to you, you must look at it as a long game, but the good news is that it can be done, and the choice is yours. "Today I will do what others won't, so tomorrow I can do what others can't." That's a quote from Hall of Fame wide receiver Jerry Rice, and I think it perfectly encapsulates what you can accomplish once you learn how to push past your comfort zone.

If you take the time to think about and analyze your fears, you'll begin to realize that they are probably all intellectual fears. You are in no real danger right at this moment. What you fear is a future that doesn't exist. Fear is a powerful force, so you must trust that freedom lives on the other side of the fear that is the boundary of your comfort zone. Instead of being afraid of your fears and allowing them to limit your potential, recognize them for what they are, and use them to grow.

If you don't know where to start, grab a notebook and a pen so you can begin journaling answers to these questions. Don't rush through it. Take your time.

Journal Prompts

- Write down a list of all your fears, and where you think you learned them.

- Now, write down the emotional pain you're anticipating for each of your fears; be honest with yourself about whether a fear is real or imagined.

- How is fear holding you back from taking the action required to get the life you want?

- How can you release any fears and take action toward the future that you desire?

- List some ways that you can turn fear on its head and use it to your advantage.

For more journal prompts and video lessons from this book, go to:
https://RobDial.com/LevelUp.

CHAPTER 2

Identity

You Aren't the Person You Think You Are

There's a great documentary called *Jim & Andy: The Great Beyond*. In it, we watch as Jim Carrey transforms into comedian Andy Kaufman when filming the movie *Man on the Moon*. Andy Kaufman was known in his acts for radically pushing the boundaries of what people thought was possible. He didn't just step over boundaries; he blew past them. Carrey is a method actor, so he remained completely in character as Kaufman for the entire four-month shoot. Even when the cameras were off and he left the set, he stayed in the role, doing everything in his power to *be* Andy Kaufman. Even the actors who had been in the TV show *Taxi* with the real Kaufman felt that Carrey was indistinguishable from the Andy Kaufman they had worked with.

When he was finished shooting the film, Carrey said he no longer knew who he was. He forgot what he believed, what made him happy or angry. He said, "At a certain point I realized, 'Hey, wait a second. If it's so easy to lose Jim Carrey, who the hell is Jim Carrey?'" This was the beginning of his spiritual awakening, and it all started by getting out of the box of who he thought he was so he could change his personal identity. He lost himself, and after greater reflection, he eventually realized that Jim Carrey was just one of the characters he was playing. Guess what? That's a good thing.

In order for a seed to grow into a flower, it must completely destroy itself. When a flower is full-grown, no part of that original seed remains. I heard that in the movie *Honey Boy* (screenplay by and starring Shia LaBeouf), and it hit home because sometimes you need to experience a breakdown to have a breakthrough. If you truly want to change, some other part of you needs to die, and that starts with the character you are playing. And we are all playing a character.

> In order for a seed to grow into a flower, it must completely destroy itself. If you truly want to change, some other part of you needs to die.

When playing a video game, you start at level one and try to get a feel for the game. You experience growing pains, struggle, and usually die multiple times. It takes a lot of trial and error, but you learn and slowly you get better until you can overcome the challenge at the end of the first level. You feel a sense of accomplishment. You don't want to keep playing level one over and over. That would be boring. You're excited to move on to level two because there will be a new set of challenges. Life works the same way. New challenges, whether chosen or imposed, force you to push yourself—to learn, grow, and change.

Tragedy aside, I've learned that life's challenges can serve a purpose by creating an opportunity. For example, the first time I played the video game called "starting a business," I was terrible at it. That business didn't succeed, but I kept trying. The second time I was definitely better, yet clearly not good enough, but the third time I played, I finally figured out what I needed to do. I used the knowledge I gained from the first two attempts to get that third business to work. I overcame the challenges and made it to the next level.

Think about how boring it would be to play a video game where you're a character who sits on the couch all day scrolling through Instagram. Nobody would ever play that video game because it doesn't have any challenges, yet that's the character so many people choose to play in life. We've all created our own character over the years. Every morning, we wake up and unconsciously decide to play that character. All we know is that character, and not being able to play that character scares us. It's that character you choose to play—your identity, or who you think you are—that is the second biggest reason after fear why you don't take action. It becomes so easy to tell ourselves a story that isn't true, but our identity, the character we embrace, can easily keep us stuck in our ways so things never change, so that we never make it to the next level.

What if instead of playing that character, you played a character that embraces challenges, and takes the action required to achieve your goals? It will make you smarter. It will make you stronger. And it will make life more fun. When we change our identity, we can change our actions, which can ultimately change the direction of our lives. The problem is that we often make the mistake of thinking we can't change.

When I discuss identity with clients, they often tell me, "That's just my personality." But what is a personality? The word "personality" derives from the Latin word *persona*, which is a mask people wear when acting onstage.[1] That mask is who we think we should be, and it influences the decisions we make. We've worn that mask for so long that we often don't realize who we really are, and we don't realize that we can take it off at any time. Writer and philosopher Alan Watts said, "You are under no obligation to be the person you were five minutes ago," which I like to think means we have the power to choose to act a different way, or put on a new persona, any time we want.

It's empowering to recognize we can change our persona, but it's also one of the hardest things to do because we are so attached to being the person we *think* we are. And the ego does not want us to think that we are anyone different. We have built so many constructs around who we think we are—man, woman, son, daughter, Republican, Democrat, athlete, parent, Christian, Buddhist, the list goes on and on.

That identity drives our actions. If you believe you are a person who is lazy and gives up easily, you'll be lazy and give up; but if you believe that you're a person who takes action and works toward your goals and dreams without ever quitting, that's exactly what you will do. Whatever you think you are, you are. Try thinking of your identity as related to actions and results, as in the following figure. Your identity influences your *actions*, which determine your *results*, which feed back into your *identity*. The problem is that most people don't have an identity that lines up with the future they want to create. And when your identity isn't lined up with the future you want to create, you will never create that future. It's a cycle, so the only way to create the future you want is to change your identity.

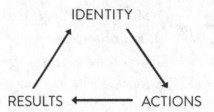

What's the Story You Tell Yourself?

Your identity is fueled by the story you tell yourself. It's that voice in your head that is always running in the background. In his 1960 book *Psycho-Cybernetics*, Maxwell Maltz referred to this as imagination. He wrote: "A human being always acts and feels and performs in accordance with what he imagines to be true about himself and his environment . . . For imagination sets the goal 'picture' which our automatic mechanism works on. We act, or fail to act, not because of 'will,' as is so commonly believed, but because of imagination."[2]

You can also think of the story you tell yourself as a song that you hear in the morning that gets stuck in your head and you wind up hearing it all day. You can change the song in your head at any moment, but most people don't and listen to that same song over and over. It's not necessarily the song you want to listen to. You might even hate it, or parts of it, but it's stuck there, and you're used to it, so it almost feels comfortable. Most people who are miserable don't want to be miserable, but they're used to the misery and are so comfortable there that they put themselves back into it every day. This is the same as the story we tell ourselves. What is that story for you?

Believe it or not, our identity distorts reality. It distorts our thoughts and feelings to the point where we see only the things that confirm what we think and feel. In other words, perception is a controlled hallucination. The technical term for this is cognitive distortion, and this includes the way we exaggerate, overgeneralize, label, filter, and think about things in terms of extremes or in black-and-white terms that don't line up with reality. These false stories we tell ourselves are almost always negative and can impact our work and relationships while holding us back from achieving our goals.

It's important to identify your story because it influences everything you do or don't do, what you think about yourself, how you feel about everyone else, the importance you place on your past, and the state of your current circumstances. That story you tell yourself is the most powerful thing in the world. And your life won't change unless that story—your identity—changes.

> Your life won't change unless
> your identity changes.

You get stuck in negative cycles when the story running in your head tells you your life looks this way because *you are this way*. If all your relationships fail, it means you believe you are someone who is bad at relationships, or you tell yourself a story that there is nobody good out there, and therefore you will eventually screw up every relationship. We all have these stories that we tell ourselves. None of them is true, but we're living our lives to line up with these stories. Why is that? It's the identity triangle. Our identity influences our *actions*, which determine our *results*, which feed back into our *identity*. We believe that's the way we are, so we take actions that line up with that identity, and those actions generate results that reinforce it.

The only way to get different results is to identify the story in your head and change it to line up with the results you want. The thing is, breaking free from that story can be terrifying because sometimes it's all we know. We do this all the time: we know we want something, but we can't do what it takes to get it. We can *want* to get in the best shape of our lives, but not do it. We can *want* to be wealthy, but not make any more money. We can *want* great relationships, but not find ourselves in them.

Why? There are two sides within our minds that are constantly at war: the conscious and the unconscious. The conscious mind wants to lose weight, eat better, and exercise so we can feel good and be healthy, but when we have a story running in our heads that says "I'm overweight," we are bombarded with thoughts like "This is who I am, and I will always be this way"; "it's in my genes, so there is no way I can change it"; "nobody in my family is in shape, so what chance do I have?"; "I'm just not athletic. If I had a different body type, it would be easier to lose weight"; "if I were taller, I would look much thinner."

If the story you're telling yourself is that you can't ever lose weight because of your genes, why even bother working out or eating healthy foods? You've already made up your mind that it's pointless. Eating fruits and veggies and working out are a hell of a lot harder than eating pizza and not working out. If my body and energy level would never change, I would never work out and I'd eat pizza all day long. Probably a ton of cookies and a lot of ice cream, too. Why would I ever want to work out if my body didn't change? So, if you think it's pointless, you have absolutely no motivation.

I'm not saying that people with certain body types don't face challenges. It's true that it can be more difficult for some people to get in shape and lose weight, but except for very rare medical conditions, there is nothing in your genes preventing you from losing weight. There are plenty of people who grew up overweight and unhealthy only to become incredibly athletic adults. The problem isn't their genes; it's that the right actions (eating a healthy diet and exercising regularly) weren't prioritized and made a habit.

For those who manage to change their bodies, it first starts with willpower. What many people don't realize is that you don't need motivation to begin. Motivation follows action, so often all you need to do is get started, and then you will create the motivation to keep going. Have you ever not wanted to go to the gym but showed up anyway, and once you started moving, you found yourself getting more excited to finish the workout? That's because taking action makes you more motivated to keep going, but you can't force yourself to take action every time. What's most important is that you are consistent, because consistency is a decision and motivation is fleeting. The conscious mind represents only 5 percent of our thoughts, while the unconscious mind makes up 95 percent.[3] That's nineteen times stronger. The unconscious mind will almost always be the default setting unless we have awareness and the intention to change it.

If you want to give yourself a fighting chance, you need to change the story you tell yourself. If you do that and start to see positive results, you can begin to change your identity. Over time, that reduces the resistance you will encounter when you need to take the actions required to achieve your goals. But if you don't ever change your story, and you continue telling yourself and others that you can't lose weight because of your genes, it will make it much harder to lose weight. You will struggle to take the action needed to lose that weight.

You may convince yourself for a little while that you want to get fit and lose weight, but a good indication that you haven't completely changed your identity yet is when you get a case of the "I deserve its." That's when you start to think, *I lost thirty pounds, so I deserve a pizza.* Then, a few days later, you might think, *I deserve to skip the gym.* Then, *I deserve some ice cream.* Through a collection of tiny decisions, it isn't long before you wake up and realize that you're back at the same weight as when you started, wondering, *How the hell did that happen?* You might have thought you had changed, but you didn't change your identity. It's still linked to your original weight, and because your results feed back into your identity, and that only further reinforces the belief that you can't lose weight, nothing changes. If that sounds familiar, you aren't alone. Between 90 and 97 percent of people who lose a significant amount of weight end up gaining it right back. No fad diet or short-term thinking is going to change your identity.

The Emotional Cycle of Change

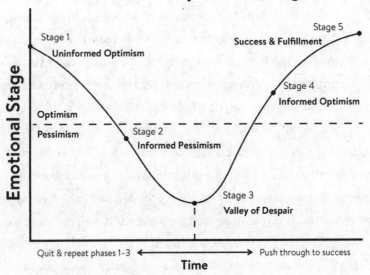

This is normal. It's part of what's called the emotional cycle of change, which was developed by Don Kelley and Daryl Conner in the 1970s, and it applies to almost anything you're trying to do differently.[4] In the beginning, you have what's called uninformed optimism. This is when life seems great because you can't see the cost. It doesn't last long and quickly devolves into informed pessimism where doubt sinks in and you understand the difficulties, so you start questioning if the change is worth the effort. It only gets worse until you hit the valley of despair, which is when most people quit because the benefits seem so far away. They then start something new, so they can return to that uninformed optimism stage when everything seems so exciting, only to go through the same cycle and quit when they reach the valley of despair all over again. That's why it's so important to push through the valley of despair by taking action. If you ride this wave long enough, it has to go up.

Nothing is good forever, and nothing is bad forever either. When you consistently take action, you gain more knowledge and experience. Just like with your video game character, you will improve, you will hit that next level, then the next, so if you keep going and commit to getting better every single day, you can't help but reach the stage of informed optimism. That's where you feel momentum and eventually succeed. You cannot fail if you don't give up.

The best way to push through is to change the way you think about your goals. For anyone who wants to lose weight, the goal shouldn't be to lose weight. The goal must be to change your identity so you believe that you are someone who is fit and healthy. Instead of looking at pictures on Instagram and saying, "I wish I had that guy's genes so I could have a body like him," you need to say, "I'm working really hard to have a body like that." Imagine how much your actions would change if your identity wasn't that of the overweight kid but of the athlete who is meticulous about the food they put in their body and the way they take care of themselves.

This applies to everything you do. You could want to grow your business, but after watching your parents destroy a business (or running a business into the ground yourself, as I did), the story you might tell yourself is that you don't have what it takes to be a successful business owner. If you believe that, running your business will be a struggle, and your story can set in motion a self-fulfilling prophecy that leads to your running it into the ground.

When it comes down to it, you are not who you think you are. Charles Horton Cooley, an American sociologist from the early twentieth century, said, "I am not who you think I am; I am not who I think I am; I am who I think you think I am." Read that one again if you have to because it's a statement that helps capture the complexity of identity. We don't create our identity on the basis of what we think of ourselves, or even of what other people think of us, but what we think they think of us.

For example, one of my good friends from high school grew up poor and always used to joke about how broke he was. He watched his parents fight about money and struggle to stay out of debt. Money was tight, and he could never get the things he wanted and was often embarrassed by what he assumed the other kids thought of him. Those experiences influenced his beliefs about money and self-worth, which led him to believe that he would always be broke. Meanwhile, he still makes broke jokes about himself today, and guess what? He's thirty-five and still broke! Why? Because that's his identity. His actions line up with the story he's telling himself. He may write off those jokes as being self-deprecating, but they're self-sabotaging and are part of what is trapping him in his current reality. If he thinks of himself as someone who will always struggle financially, the actions he takes become a self-fulfilling prophecy. He is speaking his reality into existence. That can show up in the form of not working as hard for a promotion, not saving his money, or not doing what's necessary to break the cycle.

This is the reason why up to 70 percent of people who win the lottery end up going broke a few years later.[5] It's the same with many professional athletes who come from nothing and sign massive contracts only to go bankrupt later in life. Sure, a lot of decisions can factor into these outcomes, but for many it traces back to their identity. Being successful and wealthy doesn't line up with the story they've been telling themselves their entire lives. Even though they came into a lot of money, their identity never shifted.

Like my friend from high school, I grew up poor as well. I used to make the same broke jokes right along with my friend, but when I reached my twenties, I realized that I didn't want to be broke anymore. One of the most stressful things in the world for me back then was the moment right before I looked at my bank account. I had so many overdraft fees that I had no idea whether I would have a couple hundred dollars in the bank or owe a couple hundred dollars to the bank.

I didn't want to live like that anymore, so I changed my behavior and reexamined my spending habits. I made an effort to save my money. Pretty soon, checking my bank balance stopped being stressful. As I saved more money, I started to get pleasure from watching my balance increase because I knew that I was moving toward the wealthy future I desired, so I started checking it every day. Equally important, I stopped making broke jokes. That helped me change the story I told myself from "I hope there is money in my bank account today" to "I am working hard to create the wealth that will change my life and my family's lives for the better." Checking my bank balance became a habit, and I still do it thirteen years later.

Your identity influences your actions, which determine your results, and your results will almost always line up with your identity. They not only line up with your identity; they reinforce it and make it stronger. So, if you aren't getting the results you want, it's because of your identity. If you don't have the body, money, relationships, or business you want, it's because of your identity. It's time to change that.

Changing Your Identity Begins with the Actions You Take

Thinking about who you want to be is only half the battle because nothing will change if you don't change your actions. You can sit all day and try to manifest a successful future, but you still must take action to do it. The more you take action, the more your results will begin to change, and over time, that changes your identity.

I'm used to speaking in front of large groups of people now, but that wasn't always the case. I cringe when I think back to the first speech that I gave at one of my early sales jobs. It was all about how we needed to stick together as a team, using the example of how penguins stick together. It was around Halloween, so I went to Walmart and bought a children's penguin costume that didn't come close to fitting me. Going into that speech, I was so nervous because I had never done such a thing before. My employers threw me up onstage and forced me to figure it out. While that penguin costume was definitely a disaster that I learned never to do again, after that, I took every chance I got to give speeches and lead team meetings so I could improve. By the time I left the company, I had more than twenty thousand hours of public speaking experience under my belt.

I certainly wasn't a public speaker when I started, but I took the actions of a public speaker. That's what began to change my results, and with it, my identity. As I write this, I'm excited about a speech

I'm about to give to a thousand people. The same thing happened with my podcast. I was definitely not a podcaster when I recorded the first few episodes, but I took the action of recording that first one, and now, thirteen hundred episodes later, my identity has changed to that of a podcaster. If you want to hack the system, take action toward the result that you want because your actions will get you different results, which will change your identity. It all goes back to what we learned in Chapter 1: overcoming fear and stepping out of comfort zones is where real growth occurs.

Here's what's wild: you don't even have to believe that it's going to work at first. Natalie was a client in my coaching program who didn't think she would ever be able to meet her goal of making $100,000. But she knew that if she kept building on the momentum that she had created with her new coaching business, she'd make more money and her business would grow. She worked so hard and gave her clients so much attention that she stopped paying attention to how much money she was making (which I don't necessarily recommend; you should always pay attention). But when she finally looked, she had made close to $170,000. When she wasn't paying attention, she blew past what she believed to be her limits. How you change your identity is by taking action even before you believe you can make that thing happen. Most people don't realize that and hold themselves back because they don't believe in themselves, but that doesn't matter. All you have to do is take action, and you can eventually change your identity.

Author and sports psychologist Trevor Moawad told a story of a kid who was failing high school in his junior year and hanging out with the wrong crowd. He got into trouble, showed up late to class, and sometimes skipped school altogether. He rarely did homework, and when he did, he didn't get good grades. College seemed like such a long shot that he wasn't even going to take college entrance exams because, what did it matter? His mom convinced him otherwise, so he took the SATs, and guess what? When he received his score in the mail, he got 1,480 out of 1,600, a high score for the SATs. It shocked him, and it shocked his mom too, who, on the basis of how he was doing in school, immediately thought he had cheated, but he hadn't.

When he got that score, something clicked in his head. He realized that he was smart after all, and things began to change his senior year. He took school more seriously. He started hanging out with a different crowd and didn't get into trouble anymore. Instead of skipping school, he showed up early. He started studying, so his grades improved, and people treated him differently. Suddenly, college became an option. He had done so poorly at the beginning of high school that he could get into only a community college, but then he transferred to an Ivy League school and went on to become a successful CEO of an international magazine. All of that success could be traced back to that SAT score because that's when his opinion of himself changed. That's when his identity changed—which is what's most important.

But in a twist no one saw coming, it turns out all those changes were built on a mistake. Twelve years later, he received a letter from the College Board saying that he was one in a small group of people whose test scores had been miscalculated. He didn't get a 1,480; he got a 740. The reality was that he did terribly on the test, but by the time he found out, that didn't matter. The only thing that mattered was that once he thought he was smart, his identity changed and he started taking smart actions that changed his life. He also changed the story he told himself, which then changed his actions and eventually his results, while reinforcing the identity that he was smart. All of that had nothing to do with his SAT score and everything to do with himself and the story he was telling himself about how smart he was.

This is the perfect example of how, when you change your identity, your actions change, which gives you different results, which reinforces your identity, good or bad. That's how powerful identity is, and every single person can do it.

Take a minute to think about *your* identity. What's the mask you're wearing? Are you the smart kid? The dumb kid? The business-is-hard kid? The one who struggles to succeed? Are you shy or not good enough? After you spend some time ruminating on this, ask yourself one of the most important questions that very few people ask themselves: What were you conditioned to believe during your childhood?

A client once told me, "I was never afraid of money, but I always knew that to make money I had to work very hard, and that wasn't appealing to me."

So, I asked, "Who demonized hard work for you as a child?"

It's no surprise, but it was his parents. He grew up with a father who worked hard and ran his own business but was barely around for the family. His dad missed dinners, didn't show up to baseball games, so as a kid, my client grew up believing that running a successful business meant working all hours of the day and neglecting family. Looking back, he realized that there were repeated instances (in sports, school, and work) when he gave up early in the process because hard work was necessary to get where he wanted to go. What he didn't realize was that his dad was probably showing him his love by providing the best life he could for his family, which was the only way that he knew how to do that. People tend to fall into one of two camps: one where it's all about the hustle and hard work, and the other where hard work is demonized. My client grew up in the second camp.

Luckily, I never had that issue growing up. Though I watched my father struggle with hard work, my uncle Dan was the antithesis of my dad. Dan owned a company with more than two hundred employees that produced and cut glass. He was successful and traveled all over the world. He had nice houses, boats, and cars and was also the most generous person I knew. If anybody in the family needed something, he was always there to step in and help. He was my first mentor, and he was the person I looked up to the most. I wanted to be just like Uncle Dan, and he showed me what I could become if I was willing to work for it. I cannot imagine who I would be today if I hadn't had such an amazing man to look up to as a child.

I was never actively looking for it, and I probably couldn't articulate it the same way at the time, but watching the difference between my dad and Uncle Dan, I picked up on a pattern. My dad would always say that he wanted something, but he would never actually work for it; whereas if Uncle Dan wanted something, he took action and worked for it.

Uncle Dan wasn't the only one in the family who taught me about hard work. Up until 2008, my mom worked in real estate, but when the recession hit, she went from earning decent money to earning nothing. Instead of making excuses, however, she got resourceful and figured out a solution, albeit an unconventional one: my five-foot-one-inch mother started driving an eighteen-wheel truck through all the lower forty-eight states. Yes, my mom became a truck driver. It wasn't a permanent career change, but when times got tough, she did what she had to do. When the economy recovered, she transitioned back into real estate.

What I learned from both my mom and Uncle Dan was that if I

wanted something in life, I couldn't sit around and wish for it; I had to take action to go out and get it. I bring that ethos to my work today; in fact, I love working and I love what I do so much that sometimes I have to hold myself back because I could work forever.

Follow Through with Your Thoughts and Words

If you want to change your identity, then change your actions, but start by turning your attention to your beliefs, thoughts, and words.

One of the best examples of this is a story I heard Jesse Itzler tell about Chadd Wright. Wright is a former Navy SEAL and a current ultra-runner who runs hundreds of miles. Itzler was telling Wright he had a friend who wanted to run long distances but couldn't break five miles. So Wright invited that friend to come run with him, and during his first run with Wright, Itzler's friend ran more than one hundred miles. How? With one simple secret. Wright told him to repeat two things: the first one was "I don't quit." When you say to yourself over and over that you don't quit, guess what you don't do? Quit! You keep going, so this guy pushed himself to keep going. The second thing he repeated was "Don't give your pain a voice."

Wright knew that when you run a hundred miles, you will be in pain. The trick is to not talk or think about it. Instead, think of what you're grateful for. So, he would stop every hour and make it a point to say what he was grateful for, and while running, he focused only on the positive. Chadd Wright isn't the first person to think of this; numerous studies have shown the significant impact positive self-talk can have on athletic performance.[6]

Using that simple technique, this one normal guy went from not being able to run more than five miles to running more than one hundred miles in a single session. By doing that, he was able to change his identity. It sounds so simple, but it can be difficult to do because it feels unnatural. It goes back to how we think more about what we don't want than what we do want. We must constantly work to flip that to focus on the positive. What do you want out of life, and what will life look like when you take the action to get what you want?

When I interviewed the actor Matthew McConaughey on my podcast, he told me how the third spanking he ever got was for saying "I can't." That was one thing that his parents never allowed him to say. He told me: "I learned and heard from my parents that 'can't' is a bad word. You get your mouth washed out for saying 'shit,' 'fuck,' and 'damn,' but if you say C-A-N-T, whoa, bend over."

With that attitude instilled in him at such a young age, it isn't much of a surprise that McConaughey went on to become massively successful and one of the coolest guys on the planet. Because he was never allowed to say "I can't," he grew up thinking he could do whatever he wanted. He had the identity of a superhero, and it stuck with him all his life.

Spend a Day as the Person You Want to Become

Think of how Jim Carrey playing the role of Andy Kaufman for only a few months resulted in Carrey completely forgetting who Jim Carrey even was. The same can be true for you. The person you are now is only a character you have created over the years. Not everything is a misrepresentation of your true self, but that old character is the one who has created the life you have now. If you're going to take action to create the life you want, you need to change some things, starting with your identity. It's that simple. You can't think that you're going to be overweight forever and then suddenly develop the body of an athlete. You can't think you'll never have a job you love and then suddenly land your dream job. You can't think you'll never have a close-knit group of friends and family and suddenly find yourself with an amazing support system. You must make a conscious effort. So, how about you try to release that character and become the person you truly want to become? Try on a new mask and become a new character today.

Here's a challenge. Think about your ideal self. Dream big! Create a picture of someone who already has everything you want in life. They have the relationship you want, the amount of money you want, the body you want, the family life you want, the job or business you want, and even all the joy, peace, and happiness you want. They've gone out and achieved everything that you want to achieve. Nothing is missing. In your eyes, their life is perfect.

Now, try to describe that person's typical day in as much detail as possible. When do they wake up? What is their morning routine? What do they eat? How often do they work out? Who do they surround themselves with? What does their career or business look like? How do they talk to themselves? How do they talk to others? How do they treat their friends? How do they treat strangers? Familiarize yourself with every single trait this person has and action they would take. Once you can identify everything, your goal is to start taking the actions that person takes for one entire day.

When you wake up tomorrow, spend the day as that person. Try on that mask. If you want to be wealthy, then tomorrow, spend the day as someone who is good at making money. If you want to be smarter, then tomorrow, be someone who has a thirst for knowledge. Get up in the morning when that person gets up. If that person works out and eats healthy food, guess what you'll do? If that person is more outgo-ing, make it a point to strike up a conversation with someone sitting next to you at a coffee shop or taking your order. If that person is nicer and in a more loving relationship, this gives you a chance to try that new role on for size. There is no risk in trying to be this new person for a day. You can always return to being your normal self tomorrow if you don't like it.

If you don't know what that person might do in a situation, stop and think about it. When you need to go to the gym but don't feel motivated, what would that person do? If you mess something up with your business or at work, what would that person do? If you get into an argument with your spouse, what would that person do? If your kids have a breakdown in the middle of the grocery store, what would that person do? There will probably be a lot of moments like that, and they will help you identify additional behaviors that you might not even realize are holding you back. No matter where you are and what you're doing, learn to make that person your guiding light.

Throughout the day, you will notice moments when you slip back into your old self. That's your existing identity trying to lure you back into your comfort zone. Stop yourself. The trick is being able to resist the temptation to do what's easy. You might get agitated at something that your ideal self wouldn't, so this is an opportunity to catch yourself and change that behavior. Bring that ideal version of yourself into the present moment and act like that person. This is all about stepping out of your comfort zone and doing things that will challenge you because if it doesn't challenge you, it doesn't change you. Try it out and see what it feels like to break out of your identity and put on a different mask, or persona, just for a day. Think of it like a shirt. If you like it, you can keep wearing it, but if you don't, you can try on a new one the next day. There is no harm in trying.

I'm not a very religious person, but I like to think that when we get to the end of our lives, we will meet that person we could have been had we lived up to our full potential. So, when I come face-to-face with God or whoever might be judging me, I want to have checked off every single item on that checklist that is required to be that perfect version of myself. My goal is to fully realize my potential and to have influenced the world and people around me as much as possible. I want to have been the best possible parent and steward of my money, and to have loved everyone as much as possible. If I ever get to meet that best possible version of myself at the end of my life, I don't want to be disappointed that I didn't become that person. Instead, I want to look at that person and realize that I couldn't have done any more during my time here on Earth to live up to that potential. I want to look at that person and feel like I'm looking at my twin.

This can be your new goal, and if you ever aren't sure that you're on the right track, ask yourself one question: "Is what I'm doing right now getting me closer to or taking me farther away from my goals?"

It's simple. If what you're doing now is getting you closer to your goals, keep doing it. If it's not, stop immediately. You can ask yourself this a hundred times a day if you need to, and it will help you shift your identity from the old version of yourself to the new version of yourself, so you can become who you need to become to create the life you want.

Remember, your identity influences your actions, which get you results that reinforce your identity. In other words, results are a reflection of your actions, so if you start taking actions that get you different results, you can begin to change your identity. Who you become is more important than what you need to do. You still need to take the actions to get the results and become that person, but if you can take off that old mask and change your identity, you open yourself up to a whole new world of possibilities. Put on a new mask, and you can take those actions naturally, which is why changing your identity is one of the most important things you can do to accomplish your goals and get the life you want.

Journal Prompts

- Write down the story you've been telling yourself that has been holding you back from where you want to be in life.

- We want to make sure we pull this out from the root. Identify and then write about where that story came from and how that functions in your life today. Maybe a particular person comes to mind who was a big influence in your life (positive or negative). Or maybe you can think back to a memory or experience from childhood, high school, or early adulthood that made an impact on your life.

- What are the thoughts, beliefs, and words you need to STOP thinking or saying to accomplish what you want to achieve?

- What are the thoughts, beliefs, and words you need to START thinking or saying to accomplish what you want to achieve?

For more journal prompts and video lessons from this book, go to:
https://RobDial.com/LevelUp.

CHAPTER 3

Purpose

What Do You Want?

"What do you want for Christmas?"

As fall rolled around, that's the question my mom would ask me each year. For many years, my answer was always the same: "It doesn't matter, get me whatever." She hated that vague answer and would try to get me to give her some kind of clue about what I wanted, but I didn't give her much to work with. Christmas always seemed so far away when she asked, so I always assumed that I'd figure it out later, but it never worked out like that.

Sure enough, on Christmas morning, I'd get all excited. Sometimes I had trouble falling asleep the night before, but it didn't matter how tired I was; I'd wake up my sister and race down the stairs first thing in the morning because I couldn't wait to open presents. I don't know what I was expecting, but there was very little that disappointed my ten-year-old self more than the Christmas when all I got were clothes.

The first words out of my mouth were "I didn't want clothes."

My mom just smiled because she knew that this would happen. "I asked you what you wanted, and you told me to get you whatever," she said.

Even I couldn't argue with that. That happened more than once before the lesson behind the saying "Ask and you shall receive" sank in.

Our goals work the same way. If we expect to get something in life, or if we want something, we need to have a crystal-clear understanding of what that is. The failure to reach that understanding is the third most common reason why people don't take action, after fear and living up to your identity.

If I place you next to the best archer in the world and ask you both to shoot at a target, that archer will beat you every time. But if I blindfold and spin the archer around and then ask you both to shoot at the target, you have a much better chance of hitting it because you can see it and the archer can't. It works the same way with your goals. Trying to achieve a goal without knowing exactly what it is you want is like trying to hit a target blindfolded. It's extremely difficult, if not impossible, to do. The clearer your goal, the better you can see it. So, instead of aiming blindfolded at a target, you'll be aiming as if you're looking through a rifle scope, which will significantly increase your chances of hitting the target.

What do you want? It sounds like a simple enough question, but do you have a specific answer? A lot of people know what they don't want. Some people kind of know what they want, but they aren't 100 percent sure. How can you expect to get what you want if you don't know what that is? My experience as a kid on Christmas morning made it very clear to me that you have to know what you want.

I've coached thousands of people over the years, and when I ask them what their goals are, they often tell me things like "I want to lose weight," "I want to get a good job," "I want to make more money," or "I want to improve my relationship." These are great ideas, and if you can attain these things, yes, your life will be improved. But guess what? They suck as goals. Why? Because they are super vague.

What does "lose weight" mean? How much weight do you want to lose? Are you talking five pounds or fifty? That's a big difference. If your goal is to lose weight, and you lose one pound, technically, you've achieved your goal. Congratulations! But is your life any different? Probably not. So, if you want to lose weight, be specific. What do you want your body fat percentage and muscle mass to be? Who has the type of body you want? Print out a picture of a person who has the body you want and put it on your mirror so you can look at it every day when you brush your teeth to remind yourself what you're working toward.

If you want to make more money, how much more money? How much do you want to add to your bank account? How much do you want to save and invest? If you tell yourself that you want to improve your relationship, how do you go about doing that? How can you gauge what is good or bad about your current relationship? Where do you want to be in your relationship down the road, and how do you get there?

A lot of people tell me they want a successful business, but when I ask them what "success" means to them, very few have an answer. How are you going to be successful if you don't know what success is? The problem with vague goals is that they could mean completely different things to different people. Financial freedom, peace of mind, inner peace, healthy relationships, self-sufficiency—what do these things even mean? They aren't specific. The amount of money that makes you financially free could be a step backward for someone else. You can always clarify what success looks like for you, so take the time to start doing that right now.

I've found that most people just want to do what they want, when they want, and with whom they want. When it comes down to it, people want options. And if you find taking action hard, it might be that you don't have that clear picture of what you want. It's much more difficult to motivate yourself to work hard to achieve something if you don't even know what that something is. If you're having trouble figuring that out, let's start by asking a few questions to help you determine what those specifics might be.

What's Your Reason for Being?

When we pursue things that we are passionate about, it's easy to be driven, motivated, and fulfilled. The problem is, most people live their lives without any true passion. It's not that they're depressed, but they aren't sure what they're supposed to be doing in this world. If you fall into this category, we need to fix that.

I love the Japanese concept of *ikigai*, which means "reason for being." Marc Winn is an American entrepreneur who created an *ikigai* diagram that helps show how meaning comes from the convergence of four areas of our life, which can be phrased as four questions:

1. What do you love?

2. What are you good at?

3. What can you get paid to do?

4. What does the world need?

Ikigai

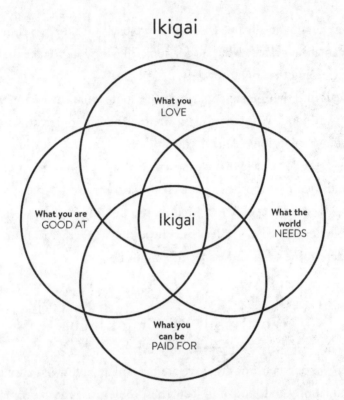

Take some time to brainstorm answers to these questions to help you narrow down your passion and purpose. Write down everything you can think of, big or small. Don't limit yourself to ideas related to business or work. If you love helping people, reading, eating ice cream, or playing with puppies, they all go on the list. Once you have your answers to all four questions, start looking for things that overlap. When you find something that is in all four categories, that is your *ikigai*, your reason to live, or your purpose.

But I want to take this a little further. There is one more question that I don't think people ask enough:

1. What are you so interested in learning or doing that you would do it for free?

Again, write down everything that comes to mind, big or small. Usually, if you find something that you're interested in, that's an indication that some sort of passion is there.

I wish that I had learned about *ikigai* earlier in my life because, even if I didn't do what I do now, I would still research humans because humans are fascinating. I love the human brain, neurology, psychology, early childhood development, and looking at someone and trying to figure how that person became who they are. That's the reason I'm so passionate about what I do. You can be passionate about something because of the result—what it will add to your life or the lives of your family members—or because of how it can impact the world.

It's perfectly okay to not yet know what your passion or your purpose is, but what's not okay is to wake up every day and not be in constant pursuit of figuring it out. You need to have a future that is so exciting that you are being pulled toward it. So much of this comes down to the future you are imagining.

Your purpose is usually right under your nose. So, how do you go about finding it? Think about it like this: Do you remember when you were a kid and thought that everything was possible? You could be an astronaut or royalty, or maybe both in the same day because, why not? Then you grew up and learned what's "realistic" and what's not, so you started holding yourself back.

Try channeling your inner child. Don't hold back; take the time to truly dream. Pretend you wake up tomorrow and receive a notification on your phone from your bank that says you have $500 million in your account. It's not a mistake. Thanks to an anonymous benefactor, you now have $500 million in the bank. What do you do now?

If you're like most people, first, you will go buy everything you ever wanted. You buy a house, and maybe multiple houses all over the world. When you have houses all over the world, you need a plane to get to them all, so you buy that. You need to get around when you're at these houses, so you buy all the cars you've ever wanted. Maybe a boat. This can go on for a while, but eventually, you will have everything you ever wanted. You might blow through $20 million, but amazingly, you still have enough left over so that you never have to worry about money again. Now what do you do? How do you spend your time?

This is when it gets a little more difficult because so many of the choices we make are about money and how to make more of it. On the one hand, it's the reality of life that in order to pay for food and shelter and clothes, we have to make money and therefore we have to work. But this often leads to our working jobs we don't love and starting businesses we aren't completely passionate about. What's great about the question "How do I want to spend my time?" is that it cuts through all of that. It takes money out of the equation and forces you to think about what it is that you truly want, which is good because human beings are capable of so much more. So many people are stuck in the rat race—they work, come home, heat up food, and sit on the couch and watch TV before going to bed and doing it all over again. The problem is that those people have grown so used to that, they don't know what to do with themselves otherwise. So instead, let's figure out what you truly want.

Go back over your answers for the *ikigai* exercise to create a list of goals, and write them down. Why write them down? Studies have shown that when you write down your goals, you make them tangible, and it becomes more likely that you will follow through and achieve them.[1] Get as clear and specific as possible—no detail is too small because you need to know exactly what you must do. For instance, instead of writing down that you want to lose weight, describe how much weight you want to lose, your desired body fat percentage, your ideal physique, and your realistic diet and exercise plan that you can stick to so you can make this change part of your identity. But knowing "what" you want is only part of the battle. We aren't done yet. We're going to take this even deeper.

The Seven Layers of "Why"

Writing down your goals may make it more likely that you will follow through, but it doesn't guarantee anything. The sad reality is people still fall short and never accomplish what they set out to achieve because they don't understand *why* they are trying to do something. In other words, you need to become emotionally attached to your goals.

When I was talking to one of my first coaching clients about his goals, he told me that he wanted to make more money. That sounded great, but it was a vague goal, so I tried to probe deeper. "Why do you want to make more money?"

"Because I want to get out of debt and be financially stable."

"That's great, but why?"

"Because I want to provide for my family."

"That's great, but why?"

This went on, and we kept going deeper and deeper. What started as that vague goal of wanting to make more money was really about how he needed to make more money because he was going through a custody battle with his ex-wife. He didn't make enough money, so his two kids lived with his ex in a less desirable part of town. We were able to uncover this subconscious fear that his children would grow up at a disadvantage, be severely hindered by the negative environment, and possibly even be in physical danger. He wanted to get his kids out of there and give them the chance to better their lives. For that to happen, he needed to make more money so he could afford a down payment on a house and regain custody. Even if his worst fears didn't come true, he knew that he would be in a position to give his kids a better chance to succeed. Accomplishing this goal could completely change the trajectory of his kids' lives. That made him work harder because he was doing it for his children. This deep level of *why* was a much more powerful driving force behind taking action than simply wanting to make more money. It wasn't about the money; it was about providing a better life for his children.

When I interviewed billionaire Jeff Hoffman, who founded Priceline .com, on my podcast, I learned that he used to do something similar with his salespeople. When they came into his office, he'd ask them what they wanted. Often, the goal would be monetary, and he'd pepper them with questions to get at the heart of why they wanted to earn more money. One employee wanted to buy a house for his mother. She had immigrated from Puerto Rico to give the family a better life and was now living in an apartment in Florida, but her dream was to own her own house. This employee wanted to make that happen.

Jeff told that employee to go find a picture of that perfect house and to tack it up in his cubicle, so he could see it every day. Whenever Jeff walked by that employee's cubicle, he would never ask about his sales numbers. Instead, he'd ask, "How close are you to getting that house for your mom?"

For both my client and Jeff's employee, the money was not the true goal. The goal was what they wanted to do with that money, and how it could change the lives of the people they cared about most. When your goal is tied to something bigger and more meaningful in your life, you don't have to work hard to get up at 5 a.m. or put in overtime. You just do it because you want to achieve the goal and know that it will change your life, and the lives of those you love.

If you're struggling to figure out what it is you want and why—what the emotional reason is behind your goal—"The Seven Layers of 'Why'" might help you better understand your purpose. Start with the first goal on your list and ask yourself, "Why?" Write down an answer, and then take it deeper by asking "why?" again. Do this seven times and see where you end up. Chances are that you will look at that goal in an entirely different light.

Once you can tap into your purpose, you will start to feel pulled toward your future—you'll be driven to achieve that goal and no longer will need to worry about motivation. What's the difference between motivation and drive? If motivation is the spark that ignites the campfire, drive is that big, dry log that burns the entire night. People believe that motivation is the secret to taking action. I get dozens of messages a day from people asking how they can become more motivated, but they don't realize they're asking the wrong question. Remember that motivation is important, and it will help you to start taking action, but drive and consistency are what allow you to keep taking action and not quit until you achieve your goal.

There is a difference between someone who is motivated and someone who is driven. You can see it in their eyes, hear it in their voice, and feel it through their body language. It's that feeling that this person will stop at nothing to do what they're trying to do. It's like those movies where a mother is searching for her missing child. That's drive. She doesn't have to work hard to pursue that goal. She doesn't have to force herself to do it. She's dedicated with every fiber of her being and doing everything she possibly can to accomplish it. She's being pulled, and that's the difference. You're at a point where there is no Plan B because it distracts from Plan A. Success is the only option.

A friend recently told me that the reason she struggles to lose weight is because she just doesn't have the time. She always plans to eat right and work out, but then life happens. Work and her children take up most of her time, so when all of that is finally handled, she's exhausted and doesn't have the energy to work out. At the end of the day, she feels like she ran out of time.

That's when I asked her, "How often do you forget to feed your kids?"

"Never!" she said, slightly offended. "Why would I ever forget to feed my kids?"

"So, it's a priority?"

"Yes, absolutely."

Working out to get healthy and live a longer life needs to become a priority for her the same way that feeding her kids is a priority, but she hasn't been thinking of it like that—and she's not alone. I constantly hear people blame their lack of time for their not achieving their goals. Does this sound familiar? That goal needs to become your priority, which seems obvious but is sometimes overlooked and is the reason why people fall short of achieving their goals.

My coach once told me to stop saying "I don't have enough time" and start saying "I don't give a damn" and see whether that changed my perception. Sorry if that sounds harsh, but it's something we all need to hear. We all make time for the things that matter, so if you're not taking the time to work out, it's because working out doesn't matter to you as much as it should. If you're not taking the time to build your business, it's because building your business doesn't matter to you as much as it should. If you're not taking the time to be with your spouse or your children and build amazing relationships, it's because family and relationships don't matter to you as much as they should.

If something is important to you, you will find a way; if something is not important, you will find an excuse.

Building the life that you want needs to become a priority, and saying "I don't have the time" is one of the biggest cop-outs you can make because it's placing blame on something external. It makes it seem like you're the victim of time, and that's not true. You are not the victim of time. You're just terrible at planning your time.

You need to step into the driver's seat and say "yes" to the life you want. You are the only one responsible for anything either happening or not happening, and the best way to push yourself to take the action required to make anything happen is by knowing what you specifically want. You are lost without your purpose. When you wake up every morning, you must focus on your purpose and allow it to pull you toward the future you want.

Journal Prompts

- If you could have ultimate success in your life, what would that mean to you? What would that feel like? Look like? Taste like? Be as detailed as possible.

- What is your most important future goal? Describe it in specific, vivid detail.

- What would it feel like to accomplish that goal?

- If you never had to worry about money, how would you spend your time?

For more journal prompts and video lessons from this book, go to: https://RobDial.com/LevelUp.

CHAPTER 4

Visualization

The Bridge to Action

When I was thirteen years old, I found myself in a championship basketball game against my friend Eddie. He was a much better basketball player than I was, and he was the best player on his team. I was the best player on *my* team, but I became incredibly nervous the night before the game. When my mom asked me whether I was excited about the game, I told her, "No, I'm scared."

My mother used to listen to the coach and speaker Tony Robbins, who at the time I thought was just some corny guy with a deep voice giving advice. I thought those tapes she listened to were silly, yet here I am today in the same business. I even got the chance to interview him twenty-three years later on my podcast. It's funny how things work out. My mom had learned about visualization from Robbins, so when I told her I was scared about the game, she said, "Just go to your room and visualize the game."

"What do you mean? How do you visualize a basketball game?" I asked.

"Just picture how you want the game to unfold. By the time you get there, it will feel like you've already done it, so you won't be scared anymore."

I lay down on the bathroom floor and started to play out the game in my head. I was probably in there for only five minutes, but it felt like thirty. That was all I needed because it worked. I can't remember if I ended up winning or losing that game, but I remember feeling much calmer because I had already been there in my mind.

Instead of being afraid of an imaginary future, I imagined a future that gave me strength. It seemed like magic, but what I didn't realize was that there was a biological reason why this was so effective. I'd later learn I had tapped into my *reticular activating system* (RAS)—a bundle of neurons in the brain at the top of the spinal column that is about the size of your little finger—which is something anyone can do. Here, let's give it a try.

Take the next twenty seconds to look around the room that you're in and count everything you see that's *red*.

I'll wait . . .

How many?

Good. Now, without looking, close your eyes and see if you can remember how many *brown* items are in that same room.

I'm sure you can remember the red items, but the brown? Not so many come to mind. Why? Because you weren't looking for things that were brown. You were looking for things that were red, and we see only what we set ourselves up to see.

At any given time, our brains can take in trillions of bits of information.[1] Right now, what can you see? What can you hear? What can you touch? Smell? Taste? The amount of information out there is overwhelming, and the brain can't process it all. Out of those trillions of bits of information, the brain can focus on only forty or fifty. It filters out the rest, and that's the job of the RAS. It's like the bouncer guarding the door of your brain. But how does the bouncer decide what to let into your brain and what to kick out? Simple. You decide, even if you don't realize it.

Here's an example. I never paid much attention to cars until I bought a new truck. I bought a Ford Raptor in a color called lead foot gray, which I had never seen before. As soon as I started driving that truck around, all I saw were other Ford Raptors, and I kept spotting more lead foot gray ones. I guess it wasn't as original as I had thought. Why? Because you don't see what you're not looking for. The opposite is true as well.

I once stumbled upon the Facebook profile of my friend Ryan, whom I went to high school with back in Florida and hadn't seen in probably a decade. I spent a couple minutes looking at his feed and then forgot about it. The next day, I was in a coffee shop and thought I saw Ryan. I almost said something, but then the guy turned around and it wasn't Ryan. But because I had been thinking about him the day before, my brain had been focusing on him, and when the brain focuses on something, it looks for answers and solutions, or in this case, tries to make connections.

When I interviewed Stanford professor and neuroscientist Andrew Huberman on my podcast, he explained how it's the job of the RAS to filter out most of the world. The chemicals in your brain guide your nervous system and divert resources to seek out and find more of what you tell it to. It is why practicing gratitude can have such a positive effect, because it increases the production of serotonin to make you feel good about other things in your environment. It's why when you're at a concert or sporting event, you can walk through crowds of people who are all talking and not hear a word. But if someone calls out your name, your head will spin around because acetylcholine and epinephrine allow you to home in on that piece of information the brain deems important.

Your RAS is also constantly looking for data and patterns that fit and validate your belief systems and identity. So, whether you realize it or not, you're the one setting the system. You're paying the bouncer and telling that bouncer what to let in based on everything you pay attention to. It doesn't matter whether it's positive or negative. If you watch the news and all you hear about is how the world is imploding, you're going to believe the world is falling apart. Who do you talk to? Who do you associate with? How do you spend your time? If you surround yourself with negativity and develop a victim mentality such that it feels like everything is happening *to* you, everything is going to keep happening *to* you instead of happening *for* you. And since the brain's default is negative, there is a good chance that very little is going to change until you intervene. But since you set the parameters, you can choose to rewrite the script and focus on something different. You can focus on the positive and what you want in life, and that is what your RAS will attempt to seek out and validate, therefore welcoming more of that into your life. It starts with the questions you ask yourself.

The brain solves problems and will always find the answers to whatever questions you ask because an unresolved question is a threat to the brain. And what is negativity? What are fear, guilt, and shame? They are all problems that need to be solved and questions that need to be answered. You're never going to get the brain to stop trying to solve problems and answer questions, so don't even try. That's a losing battle. But instead of trying to fight that battle, you can change the questions you ask yourself. When you do that, you change how you feel, and that will reverberate through everything you do and make you more inclined to take action. It's the beginning of a positive feedback loop.

Here's how it works: Let's say you're quitting your job to start your own business, but you're worried about money and being able to get out of the starting gate. Those are reasonable concerns, so you start asking yourself questions like "Am I going to go broke?" and "What could go wrong that I'm not thinking of?" And if you are wondering what could possibly go wrong, your brain will work harder than Google to search for all of the different things that will go wrong. That becomes what you focus on, so the RAS does its job to make it more likely that something will, in fact, go wrong because that's what you are searching for and the RAS will make sure you always find what you're searching for.

You need to flip the script. Instead, ask yourself, "What makes this the right time to quit my job?" or "How am I qualified to run this business?" Focus on positive questions. Write them down; make them a mandatory part of your journaling practice. The important thing is to get yourself asking questions that your brain can't help but find answers to that will be positive in your life.

Let's say your identity has been shaped around the idea that you aren't worthy of success. Instead of asking yourself "Am I going to fail?," flip the script and ask, "Why do I deserve to be successful?" or "What good can I do with my success?" or "How will my success improve life for my family and me?"

Let's say that you fear you're a bad parent. Get your brain thinking the opposite through questions: "What can I do today to improve the lives of my children?" "How am I being there for my kids today?" "How can I lean into my biggest strengths as a parent?"

It's all about keeping your eyes on the prize and remaining focused on where you want to go so that you will attract that future and be able to recognize all of the opportunities when they present themselves. The questions will change your focus and your focus will dictate how you feel, but you can take that a step further. Like my mother knew before that basketball game, one of the best ways to set your brain to create and feel pulled toward the future you want is through the power of visualization.

Normalizing the Future You Want

When I visualized my championship basketball game when I was thirteen, I wasn't stumbling upon anything new. Athletes had been doing that for years, and some of the top athletes still practice visualization. This isn't woo-woo stuff; multiple scientific studies show how visualization (or mental imagery) can increase sports performance. It's been shown to help improve athletes' motor skills and enhance their ability to learn new skills during practice. For instance, a study published in 2017 showed visualization to be more effective at improving athletic performance than relying on external factors to provide motivation.[2] The key is to focus not only on the outcome, but also on the process.

Human beings are very much a species driven by results and facts. We want proof that we can do something before we try to do it. If we don't have that proof, it's harder for us to take action. The brain is afraid of doing what it hasn't done before. This makes sense because the brain is trying to protect us, but it also creates limitations that don't exist.

Before 1954, everyone thought it was impossible to run a mile in fewer than four minutes. Nobody had done it. Experts, and even doctors, said it was physically impossible. People thought the human heart might explode if people pushed themselves that hard. Since the experts, the people who supposedly knew best, were saying this, that's what most people believed—until Roger Bannister came along. In 1954, Bannister ran a mile in 3 minutes and 59.4 seconds. He proved that the impossible was possible.

What's crazy about this story is not that Bannister ran a sub-four-minute mile; it's that over the next two years, three hundred people also did it, with the second person doing it about three months after Bannister. How is that possible? Did humans magically evolve as a species to become stronger and faster between 1954 and 1956? Did their lung capacity change? Absolutely not. What changed was how they perceived their limitations. The ability to run a mile in fewer than four minutes was always there, but the belief was not, and that's what held so many people back.

People used to look up at the sky, watch the birds, and think of how amazing it would be if humans could fly—but that would never happen because it's impossible. Then, in 1903, a plane built by the Wright brothers proved the impossible possible.

People thought it was impossible for humans to ever go into space. Then, in 1961, Russian cosmonaut Yuri Gagarin was the first person in space.

People thought it was impossible to put a human on the moon, but then in 1969, Neil Armstrong became the first person to walk on the moon.

Can you honestly say that we are capable of sending a rocket with people in it more than two hundred thousand miles away to land on a rock that's orbiting the Earth at more than two thousand miles per hour, and then get it to take off from that rock and land safely back on Earth with technology that is not nearly as powerful as the smartphone we carry around in our pockets, but you can't accomplish your goals? That doesn't make any sense.

Think of the story you're telling yourself about why you can't create that business or become successful. It's a lot easier to listen to those limitations because they are safe, they are in your comfort zone. It's easier for us to sit on the couch and scroll through Instagram or watch TV because we'd be wasting our time trying to do something that's impossible. Those perceived limitations give us an excuse to not take action. They give us an excuse to not do hard things. That becomes another story we tell ourselves and another way we're programmed. It's another part of our identity or the illusion of who we believe ourselves to be. We get stuck in our heads, which is one of the many ways we hold ourselves back.

Visualization mentally prepares you to execute an action because it tricks your mind into thinking that what you're trying to do is possible. By tricking your brain into thinking you have the life you want, it makes it easier to take action toward that life.

Think about it like this: If you make $60,000 a year and then change jobs, there's a pretty good chance that you're not going to make less than $60,000 ever again because you know that you're worth it. And when you know that you're worth it, guess what you won't do? Accept anything less. That becomes your new standard. Visualization is an invaluable tool that can help you jumpstart that process by raising the standards in your mind. But don't stop there. You can take one more step, so you not only envision the future you want but can make what might initially seem out of reach feel normal.

The future goal is what you visualize, but the fruit you will bear from that accomplishment is what you can normalize. So, if your goal is to run a successful business, you visualize how that accomplishment will unfold and what it feels like. Once you have that success, you normalize what you can do, and that will be unique to you.

For years, my girlfriend (now wife) and I had been talking about moving to Rome for six months, and in 2016, we finally decided to make it happen the following year. Part of me didn't know whether it was even possible. My business was getting off the ground, and I had just bought a new house, so I had to make a lot of arrangements; but I really wanted to go to Rome, so I stopped making excuses. At the start of 2017, I became committed to moving by July 1. That was my new number one goal, and I became hyper-obsessed. I not only visualized this future goal every day, but I intensified the visualization by incorporating all five senses.

The first thing I did was pin down exactly where in Rome I wanted to live. I joined a Facebook group called Expats in Rome, and once I started communicating with people in the area about what we were looking for, I got a bunch of recommendations and picked out an area called Trastevere. I used the street view on Google Maps to "walk" the streets of this new neighborhood, which became a whole new level of visualization. I found a coffee shop in that neighborhood, and since I was drinking coffee every morning at home in Austin, Texas, anyway, I visualized drinking it in that Roman coffee shop to enhance the experience through taste and smell. I brought sound into the equation by putting on headphones and listening to a recording called "The

Sounds of Rome." So, every morning, I visualized myself walking down the streets of Rome and going to a coffee shop. In my mind, I sat outside in Rome and drank my coffee while in fact I sipped it at home with my headphones on, listening to the street sounds. I was seeing it in my head, tasting the coffee in my mouth, smelling it, listening to the sounds of the streets through the headphones, and feeling the mug in my hands and my body in the seat. I became excited to wake up every morning and use all five of my senses to experience being in Rome.

Not only does this trick your brain and body into thinking a goal is possible, but this makes you excited to take action. It gets your brain to focus on a possibility instead of defaulting to focus on problems. After doing this every day for months, visualizing all of the wine and food and smells and sounds, I was so excited to go to Rome that I couldn't wait until July 1. All of the doubts that had been in the back of my mind and problems I anticipated no longer seemed like big deals. I was eager to do the work necessary so we could leave a month earlier instead. I went from not knowing whether the move was possible to feeling like we had to get there sooner because I was so excited. It wasn't hard work or a struggle. Instead, I was being pulled toward the future I wanted.

This is called normalization, and I learned about how powerful normalization can be years ago, before I had any clue that's what I was doing. Uncle Dan lived in a beautiful, gated community in Siesta Key, Florida. When I visited him as a kid, I would ride around in their golf cart with my cousin and look at all of the huge houses. I would tell myself repeatedly, *I'm going to live in a house like that one day. I'm going to live in a house like that one day. I'm going to live in a house like that one day.* I didn't realize the significance at the time, but

I was normalizing the feeling of being around massive houses on the beach with beautiful views and Ferraris in the driveways.

When I first moved to Austin a few years ago, I didn't live in the best neighborhood and wanted to move to a nicer one eventually. Before I found the right neighborhood and house to settle down in, I wanted to normalize the feeling of living in a great neighborhood, so I used positive visualization as a tool. I would drive around those neighborhoods and pay close attention to what it felt like to navigate the streets and what the houses looked like. The point of these excursions wasn't about admiring how nice the cars or houses were in a materialistic sense, but instead about normalizing living life in such neighborhoods by experiencing part of it.

Today, I live in one of the neighborhoods I used to explore and dream about.

A friend of mine in Austin took that to the next level. He knew which part of the city he wanted to live in and one day drove by a huge modern house that was still being built. It was a weekend, and the construction crew wasn't there, so he pulled over and walked around the site. There was a pool and a great view of downtown Austin through the hills. That was his dream house. He wanted to live there, so every day after work, he drove to that house while telling himself, *I'm driving home. I'm driving home. I'm driving home.* He visualized himself living in that house and walking through the rooms. Over time, he normalized the feeling of living in a house like that.

Eventually, construction was finished, and someone bought the house. A few years later, my friend saw that it was on the market, so he tried to buy it. He was told he didn't qualify for the loan, but he didn't give up. He kept thinking positively. *This is my house. This is my house. This is my house.* In sixty days, he built his business to the point where he could qualify for the loan and bought that house four years after he had first started visualizing it. You can call it a coincidence, but I think something much deeper happened.

What do you want? Do you want to be in a great relationship, but your identity has led you to believe that it's impossible to be in a healthy and loving relationship since the relationships you saw as a child were the opposite? Go hang out with people who are in those healthy and loving relationships you desire. You will learn and normalize how relationships should be.

Do you want to be a better parent but don't quite believe 100 percent that you can be a great parent because of something that was programmed into you during childhood? Go hang out with a pair of phenomenal parents to normalize the feeling of being a good parent. Do you hope to one day own a Porsche? Go test drive one. Do you want to live in a specific city or part of town? Rent an Airbnb in the area.

No matter what the goal, it's important to incorporate all five senses into the visualization process to make it a richer experience. Let's say you want to live on the beach. Start by visualizing drinking your coffee there every morning while taking in your new view of the ocean (using your imagination for now!). If it's warm, sit outside and feel the sun on your skin. You could buy a candle that smells like the ocean and listen to sounds of the ocean through headphones. Visualization is important for the mind, but putting it into practice in the real world incorporates the body. To truly change your identity, you need to bring both the mind and the body into the equation. The story you tell your mind and the actions you take with your body are a potent combination that can help you begin to change your identity and pull yourself toward the future you want.

No matter what the goal, it's important to
incorporate all five senses into the visualization
process to make it a richer experience.

Make visualization a daily habit. Take ten minutes every day to
visualize the future you want. If you've never done this before, here's
the process that I find helpful:

1. Start by taking six deep breaths.

2. Next, it's important to bring emotion into the experience so that
   your brain and body are both present. I've done this practice with
   many different groups of people, and I've learned that gratitude is
   the most potent feeling that you can utilize to help create that sense
   of heightened emotion. Think of someone or something you love,
   and then bring all those feelings of happiness and joy to the visualization process. It's not uncommon for people to get emotional
   when visualizing their future and feeling immense gratitude as if
   they already have it. If you can fear the future, you can also feel
   grateful for it. Learn to train yourself to feel gratitude for a future
   that hasn't happened yet.

3. Get crystal clear in your mind exactly what you want and what you
   plan to both visualize and normalize.

4. Now, imagine that scenario, with lots of sensory detail so it feels
   like you're really there.

5. Repeat this process every day to hardwire it into your brain. You
   will start to notice your feelings change from "I want *XYZ*" to "I
   will have *XYZ*." When this occurs, you're being PULLED toward
   your future.

> Learn to train yourself to feel gratitude
> for a future that hasn't happened yet.

When you picture the future you want, you will feel attached to those accomplishments. You can feel proud and excited that you built this life.

You Draw Energy from the Future You Imagine

If you notice a feeling of excitement as you practice positive visualization, it's because you're envisioning an exciting future. If you are feeling discouraged, that your dream future is unattainable, it's probably because you're envisioning all of the negative possibilities the future might hold. You choose what you focus on.

I consult with many business owners in various industries at my in-person events and masterminds and have discovered that the most important factor for success for any business is the mindset of the business owner. If the owner's mind isn't in the right place, the business won't continue down the right path, no matter the industry. When I ask business owners why they feel anxious, I tend to hear the same answers: "What if I sign a client and I don't get them the results they want?" "What if someone says, 'No'?" "I'm worried about growing my business and having to build a team." "What if I have to fire someone?"

These fears and attitudes manifest in their body language. Often when they are talking about this subject, their whole demeanor changes. The reason is because we pull energy from the future we imagine. So, if you're feeling anxious, it's probably because you imagine a future that's stressful.

Imagine that you're having a dream about walking through the jungle when you spot a tiger a hundred feet in front of you. You stop and try not to make a sound. At first, it doesn't see you, and it looks like it's about to walk in the opposite direction, but right when you think you're safe, it makes eye contact. It stares at you for a moment, and then it takes off running directly toward you. You turn and bolt, but the tiger quickly gains ground. Pretty soon, you can hear it right behind you. You can almost feel its breath. You peek back over your shoulder, and see it leap up in the air. Its jaws open, and right when it's about to clamp down, you wake up in bed. It takes you a moment to get your bearings, but you're out of breath, sweating, and your heart rate is through the roof, yet you didn't move. You were lying in bed the entire time, but your physical body reacted as if the scenario you dreamed about was real. The mind literally creates those feelings in the body from the imagination alone. As author Maxwell Maltz said, "Your nervous system cannot tell the difference between a real experience and one that is vividly imagined." But this doesn't happen only when we're asleep.

As I sit at my desk writing this, I can fast-forward in my mind and picture a future where I grow an incredible business only to run it into the ground. What's crazy is that I can feel those feelings associated with the failing business in the current moment because my body releases cortisol, adrenaline, and other chemicals to make that possible. Take a second to understand how amazing this is. You can build a future that doesn't exist and make yourself feel anxious in the present moment when there is no immediate threat, like we learned in Chapter 1.

Humans are the most incredible complex beings on our planet. We have the amazing capability to create our own futures on the basis of what we imagine. The irony is that we're using our brain incorrectly because we spend more time focusing on what we *don't* want than on what we *do* want. That makes taking action much more difficult, and it's the reason why so many people end up imagining a future they fear and are trying to avoid. Who would want to take action toward a future that seems stressful? It doesn't matter what future you imagine; you will draw energy from that future and feel it in the present moment, so you need to become incredibly aware of what future you're imagining.

> It doesn't matter what future you imagine;
> you will draw energy from that future
> and feel it in the present moment.

Successful people are able to envision the future they want and not dwell on all of the things that they don't want to happen, or fear could ruin them. When you learn to turn off or turn down that part of the brain that envisions a negative future, you can then harness the power of visualization to draw energy from what you want to happen by getting clear about what your drives, motivation, and goals are.

Make it a point to keep thinking about all of the things you want to happen in the future. Picture how proud you will be when you build that business. Think about how you can positively impact the world and provide for your family because that will change the energy in your body, so instead of preventing you from taking action, it will pull you toward that future you want. When people grasp this concept, I've watched how it helps them step out of their comfort zones and begin taking action toward the incredible future they want.

> Picture how proud you will be when
> you accomplish your goals.

Journal Prompts

- What does your ideal future look like? What would you do? When would you do it, and with whom?

- What will you focus on to set your reticular activating system (RAS) to make sure you find what you're searching for?

- What fruit will accomplishing your future goal bear?

- How can you incorporate all five senses into your visualization process?

For more journal prompts and video lessons from this book, go to: https://RobDial.com/LevelUp.

Part II

HOW TO TAKE ACTION

Now that you understand why fear, the story you're telling yourself, and a lack of clear purpose are holding you back from taking action, and you have some tools to remove the mental obstacles standing in your way, we can discuss strategies to get you closer to the life you want.

In Chapter 3, you created a list with a specific goal or goals you want to work toward. Although it's good to have long-term goals, it's a mistake to focus exclusively on where you want to be in five, ten, or twenty years. It can be so daunting to think about everything you must do and how long you have to do it that it's easy to become paralyzed and do nothing. From here on out, you're going to focus on the little things. Focus on the daily actions—the micro-actions—that you can do to get you where you need to go. I like to call these *action-based goals* because the first goal is to take the daily action necessary to reach the bigger goal. These daily micro-actions feel manageable. They will create momentum and a sense of accomplishment, which will lead to sustained action. Before you know it, you'll have accomplished what you set out to do.

One of my favorite quotes about how to take action comes from James Clear in his book *Atomic Habits*: "Every action you take is a vote for the person you wish to become." That's focusing on what needs to be done, the micro-actions in the short term. That means asking yourself what you need to do today—or to make it even simpler, in the next thirty minutes—to achieve your goals. Thinking about the next step is much more realistic than thinking about the next ten years.

Achieving your goals is like going on a journey. Once you know where you're headed and what you need to do (Chapter 5), you want to clear the debris in front of you and grease the tracks to make that journey as smooth as possible. That involves learning how to eliminate distractions from your life so you can get done what you need to do. You don't even realize it, but you've been training yourself to be distracted your entire life, so it will take some work to get out of those bad habits. But it is possible, and I'll show you how in Chapter 6.

Once the distractions are cleared, when it's time to get moving, you're going to start small so you can build momentum with small wins from the moment you wake up. Becoming more self-aware of your actions and what you need to do helps ensure that you can fill your days with level-up activities that bring you closer to achieving your goals, which we'll cover in Chapter 7. Often, the area people need the most help with is focus. It's so hard to sit down for even twenty minutes and get things done without getting distracted. I will teach you how to improve and master your focus in Chapter 8, so you can consistently be productive every day.

CHAPTER 5

Direction

Set Your Internal GPS

I have something I call Living in the Headlights. It goes like this: My close friend Mike lives in Houston, which is a two-hour drive away from where I live in Austin. When I visit him, I almost always drive at night. Before I set out in my car, I can't see that destination from Austin, nor can I see every turn I will take along the way. Since it's dark, I can't see much more than the next hundred feet in front of me, so that's what I focus on. Once I get past those first hundred feet, I focus on the next hundred.

You must approach life the same way. You can't see ten years from now, three months ahead, or even tomorrow. All you can see is today, so you must do what you can to get 1 percent better today. In other words, focus only on those hundred feet that are in the headlights ahead of you. Once you move those hundred feet, there will be another hundred feet, and then another and another.

The fact that you haven't been taking action in the past doesn't matter. What matters is where you are right now, and where you want to go. Stop stressing about the future. Forget about all the success, happiness, joy, and peace you want for yourself in the next ten years, one year, or even the next month. Focus instead on leveling up today. There is no other day except for today, and that's how you should live because every day is today. You want to live in the headlights and move the needle as much as possible *today*.

> The fact that you haven't been taking action in the past doesn't matter. What matters is where you are right now, and where you want to go.

In Chapter 3, you worked on clarifying what your purpose is and what goals you need to achieve to have the life you want. Now that you have that purpose and those specific goals in mind, it's time to get going. An old proverb says that the journey of a thousand miles begins with a single step, and you can't take a second step until you take the first. If you aren't taking action, it's often because you're focused on a step very far down the road and all the steps required to reach that point, but that doesn't matter right now. What matters right now is step one. Then you can focus on step two, step three, and so on.

The direction you are heading is more important than the speed you're going. If you point yourself in the right direction and begin moving in that direction, you will eventually get there. You're going to encounter obstacles along the way, and how fast you're going will determine how quickly you'll get there, but even if you're moving slowly, you will eventually arrive at your destination.

> The direction you are heading is more important than the speed you're going.

Goals work the same way, and three components are required to make sure that you achieve them:

1. Direction

2. Action

3. Time

Focus on these three things, and I promise you will get where you're going. But you first have to know exactly where you're going.

Direction: What's Your Destination?

If you use a GPS system in your car, it needs two pieces of information: (1) where you are, and (2) where you want to be. The GPS creates a route, and that's how you get from A to B.

Life works the same way—you need to determine who you need to become, and what you need to do to get there—and that route is determined by the destination you set and the actions you take. That is the gap.

1. WHO YOU NEED TO
BECOME

2. WHAT YOU NEED TO
DO

Take a moment to think about what "destination" you are heading toward. Once that's clear, the next step will help you plot the route.

Action: Start, Stop, Continue

Once you've entered into your GPS your destination—who you need to become—you must step on the gas. Even if you're going only one mile per hour, you're moving forward and that's all that matters.

One simple practice that can help you plot the route to your destination and take action is to set aside ten minutes during the week—Sunday nights or Monday mornings work best for me—to look back at the previous week and look forward to the week ahead. Ask yourself three questions:

1. What do I need to *start* doing this week?

2. What do I need to *stop* doing this week?

3. What do I need to *continue* doing from last week?

Start. Stop. Continue. These don't have to be big things. They are the tiny adjustments that are so important because your life usually doesn't change with massive shifts. It's the little shifts that, when done every day, level you up—when you realize you did something wrong (or could be doing something better) and get back on track.

It's the micro-actions that you take every day, in the next hour or even the next thirty minutes, that make all of the difference. Keep these actions simple and focus on those moments and adjustments that will get you back on course.

So, what's the first step you're going to take today to bring you closer to your goals? Write it down.

Time: It's a Long Game

Direction and action are more important than the speed you're going, because if you're going in the wrong direction or not moving at all then it's impossible for you to arrive at your destination.

The reality is that changing your life takes time. There is no way around that. You just have to accept it. A husband would never say to his pregnant wife, "I know this is supposed to take nine months, but do you think we can hurry it up and do it in five because it would be pretty cool to get a vacation in by the end of the year?" People would think that guy's nuts because everyone knows most pregnancies last nine months.

Our goals work the same way. If you're going in the right direction and taking the actions necessary to get where you want to go, the time will work itself out. You don't have to take huge strides every day. Success is about doing the small (sometimes boring) things over and over. It's about getting just a little bit better every day. You want to go to sleep at night knowing you're better and closer to your goals than you were when you woke up that morning, even just a little bit. All you have to do is consistently get 1 percent better than you were yesterday.

I know you want to have the life you want right now, but it takes time. If you make sure that you're heading in the right direction, and taking the right action, no matter how small, you will eventually end up where you want to be. Slow and steady wins the race.

Life Can Be Easy Now and Hard Later, or Hard Now and Easy Later

Why is it so hard to make the right choices in the moment? The reason is because it's so easy to choose instant gratification over delayed gratification. Eating a cheeseburger tastes good, at least in the moment. When we're done, we might feel tired, bloated, and lack energy for the rest of the day, but there is instant gratification in that moment. And unfortunately, we have grown so used to instant gratification that it has become harder for us to wait for any reward.

I'm only thirty-six now, but when I was a kid sitting around with my friends, asking the big questions like how far the sun is away from the Earth, we couldn't just pull out our phones, type the question into Google, and get an answer in seconds. We had to hop on our bikes, ride down to the library, and track down the encyclopedias. Hopefully, the *S* volume would be there so we could look up the section on the sun and see that it ranges, depending on the time of year, from 91.4 million miles from Earth to 94.5 million miles. If the *S* wasn't there, we probably wouldn't be able to find out the answer.

Today, we've been trained to expect instant gratification because so much knowledge and convenience is available at our fingertips. If

I'm in a hurry to learn how far the Earth is from the sun, I don't even have to pick up my phone or get out of my seat. I can just ask Siri and immediately have the answer. If I'm inclined to buy something, I can get it the next day—sometimes even that same day—from Amazon. If I want to go somewhere, Uber or Lyft will send a car to my doorstep in minutes. If I'm hungry, I don't have to leave the house or turn on the oven because Postmates and DoorDash will deliver food from a restaurant of my choosing.

Technology can be great because it makes life easy and convenient, but the downside is that it has trained us to expect instant gratification. Success is one of the few things that you can't get through instant gratification; it requires consistent action. Nobody expects to go to the gym once and leave with six-pack abs. The body, business, or relationship you want isn't going to be achieved as quickly as a Google search. They all require delayed gratification, so you must learn patience, or how to be the tortoise and not the hare.

> The body, business, or relationship
> you want isn't going to be achieved
> as quickly as a Google search.

Life is hard. Nobody gets through this human experience without a few scars, but people often make it harder on themselves in the long term than necessary. What's great is that we actually have a choice: life can either be easy now and hard later, or hard now and easy later.

Do you think you're lazy? You're not. You're choosing to be lazy. Do you think you're a procrastinator? You're not. You're choosing to procrastinate. It sounds small, but one is an identity statement, and the other is a choice, and as we know from Part I, if your identity is that you're lazy and a procrastinator, you will take the actions that line up with that identity. You can always decide to do something different. There is a moment of choice before every action you take. Even if you're just lying on the couch and not doing anything, that is an action and it's a choice. There are downstream consequences to lazy choices, however, because that means choosing to make things easier now and harder later. Eating healthy food is hard now, but so is being overweight later. Having difficult conversations to repair your relationship with your spouse is hard now, but so is divorce later. Practicing financial discipline is hard now, but so is not being able to buy what you need later.

You know what's hard? Working to grow your business. You know what's also hard? Being broke. I was twenty-four when my first business failed. I was five months behind on my car payment, so I had to call my bankers and beg them not to repossess my car. I know that being broke is hard, and hard work is hard. I've done both and know that I would much rather work hard than be broke.

That's when I made a decision to change things and shift my identity. I realized that success did not have to involve working myself into the ground. I didn't have to do everything myself, so I learned how to delegate and trust people. But most important of all, I found something I was truly passionate about—my *ikigai*—which meant that I could work extremely hard pursuing what I loved without it ever feeling like work. That made all the difference. Looking back on the past twelve years, I'm glad that I put in the hard work to get where I am today. That was a choice.

With each action and with each choice, you're deciding whether or not to move the needle closer to your desired destination. The choice is yours, but keep in mind that when you choose to make things easy now and hard later, you're not only making it hard on yourself. Your choices can affect others.

An overweight man came up to me after a speaking event and told me how hard it was for him to lose weight, work out, and be healthy. I asked him, "If you can't make the lifestyle change now, what do you fear will happen in ten or twenty years?"

He said, "I'm afraid that if I die early because I'm overweight, I won't be able to walk my daughter down the aisle at her wedding or play with my grandchildren."

I asked, "If you think about it in terms of pain, what hurts more: the discipline required to eat right, exercise, and become healthy, or the real possibility that you won't be able to walk your daughter down the aisle and play with your grandchildren?"

"I never thought of it like that," he said. "But not being able to walk my daughter down the aisle is much more painful than the lifestyle change I'll have to get used to."

"So, try connecting to that thought," I said. "The next time you want to give yourself an excuse not to eat right or exercise, remind yourself of that future pain and see if that motivates you to take action." It was a small shift in perspective, but incredibly profound for him.

Six months later, he emailed me to say that he had lost thirty-five pounds. And it was all because he realized that the future pain of not being there for his family was worse than the present pain of making a lifestyle change. The hard now is never as bad as the hard later. If you buckle down and put in a little sweat now, you will be rewarded. That man chose delayed gratification over instant gratification. Instead of things being easy now and hard later, as he was living, he chose to make things hard now and easy later. That's what made all the difference and what led to real change that has him on the path to the life he wants.

> Life can either be easy now and hard later
> or hard now and easy later. You choose.

We all experience similar moments of choice throughout the day. What are the areas of your life where you're choosing things to be easy now? How will those choices make life harder in the future?

Depending on your situation, you might have to give something up. In his book *Think and Grow Rich*, Napoleon Hill lays out six steps to take to achieve your financial goals. The first is to figure out the exact amount of money you desire, and the second is to figure out what you will have to sacrifice to get it. Although he's talking specifically about money, sacrifice can apply to any goal you're trying to achieve because it acknowledges the simple fact that there are trade-offs in life. You don't have room to do it all. Something will have to go, because when you say "yes" to something, you're also saying "no" to something else. However, when you've found your purpose and spend your time working toward your goals, it's well worth the sacrifice when you can sit back and watch that lifelong dream come to fruition.

*   *   *

The journal prompts below will help you set your internal GPS. Once you're crystal clear on the direction you're heading, and the actions you need to start, stop, and continue to get there, you next want to make it as easy on yourself as possible. You will encounter obstacles and resistance, but some simple techniques can help you clear those obstacles from your path and push through the resistance.

Journal Prompts

- What are your goals regarding your destination? What action do you need to take, no matter how small, to start your journey toward that destination?

- What do you need to stop, start, and continue doing to get there?

- In what ways will life be hard now and easy later when it comes to achieving those goals?

- What, if anything, will you need to give up in order to achieve your goals?

For more journal prompts and video lessons from this book, go to: https://RobDial.com/LevelUp.

CHAPTER 6

Distraction

The Enemy of Action

Becoming a pro athlete and competing on a national stage is difficult no matter what the sport. It requires years of hard work, dedication, and practice, but few sports require the precision, patience, and focus of golf. Nobody knows this better than Rory McIlroy.

In 2011, twenty-one-year-old McIlroy was already being touted as the next Tiger Woods. He was on fire going into the Masters, the most prestigious of the four major tournaments, and was in the lead going into the final round on Sunday. He even had a four-stroke lead heading into the back nine, and it looked like he was going to cruise to a win. But then something happened. He completely fell apart. One bad shot led to another, and by the time he got into the clubhouse, he had racked up one of the worst-ever final-day rounds in tournament history and finished tied for fifteenth place.

What happened was the pressure became too much, and McIlroy admitted to losing his focus and getting distracted. Nothing else changed. He wasn't injured. He didn't suddenly forget how to play. He was simply distracted, so he got rattled and didn't perform up to his potential. That was the only difference between a tournament win and a disastrous result.

Succumbing to distraction isn't a fate reserved for professional athletes when playing on the biggest stage. It's something we all do. In fact, we've been training ourselves to be distracted our entire lives. Think about it this way: Let's say that you've never played basketball before, but you've come across a bunch of money that has set you up for life and you've decided that you want to dedicate your life to getting good at basketball. So, every day for the next five years, you practice for sixteen hours a day. During that time, all you do is eat, sleep, and play basketball. Even if you've never played before, you're going to get extremely good. You might not be a pro, but you will be significantly better than when you started. It would be almost impossible not to if you practiced that much.

We can master almost anything we spend a lot of time doing, and this is exactly what you've been doing with distraction. Whether or not it adds up to sixteen hours a day, from the moment we get up in the morning to the moment we go to bed at night, we are bombarded with distractions. Whether they come from advertisements, our phones, apps, Instagram, Facebook, TikTok, Twitter, television, email, music, notifications, our children, or other people, we can't help but give in and indulge in distraction. It happens over and over every day.

This is how we've become professionals when it comes to distraction. It's also why people have such a problem with boredom. We've become addicted to the stimuli that come from watching television or endlessly scrolling through social media. Is there anything wrong with sitting and doing nothing? No, not at all! Our brains are wired to use this "down" time to generate new ideas and work through problems. Studies have shown that simply going for a walk (especially outdoors in nature) can help calm the nervous system and create a more relaxed mood.[1] Without realizing it, we have trained our brains to go, go, go, go, go all the time, which means that the idea of sitting down and doing nothing makes us feel uncomfortable or even feels like torture! In fact, a 2014 study revealed that 67 percent of men and 25 percent of women would rather receive an electric shock than sit alone with their thoughts for fifteen minutes.[2] We've grown so used to constant stimulation that we don't know how to sit still and be alone, even for just a little while.

Marketing experts say that the average American sees between four thousand and ten thousand advertisements every day.[3] They check their phones 344 times every day. That means if you're awake for sixteen hours, you're checking your phone every three minutes.[4] The average person spends two hours and twenty-five minutes on social media every day. So many things are vying for our attention every moment throughout the day that it's no mystery our attention spans aren't what they used to be. Studies have shown that human attention spans have grown shorter in the digital age.[5] There is no denying that people are more distracted today than ever, but many don't realize how those distractions are killing their productivity and making it more difficult for them to take action toward the goals they want to achieve and the lives they want to live. If you can learn how to eliminate distractions so you can focus on the actions necessary to move the needle, you will develop what feels like superhuman productivity. That's what I will teach you how to do in the next section.

Not everyone is born with the same level of focus, but you can always improve that level of focus. How? The same way we all do: through practice. If we got ourselves into this mess, we can get ourselves out. The problem is that most of the time we don't even know when we're distracted. The first step is to better understand the enemy we must fight. It's hard to take action until we remove distraction, but once we become more aware of the various ways we're distracting ourselves, it's much easier to change our behavior. Let's take a look at the most common distractions and how to deal with them: our cell phones, notifications, other people, our physical environment, and our social environment.

Cell Phones

The cell phone, notably the smartphone, is an amazing technological advancement that has revolutionized the way we live. So much so that the average person spends three hours and forty-three minutes a day on their phone. That's a long time.

> The average person spends three hours and forty-three minutes a day on their phone. That's a long time.

Although it may be one of the most amazing pieces of machinery ever built, it's also the most distracting. It was designed that way. The more time you spend on apps, the more money companies make, so they want you on that phone as much as possible. And they do their job well because they understand how your brain works better than you do. They hire the best psychologists and neurobiologists to help them engineer apps that are psychologically and biologically addicting. They are literally exploiting the natural tendencies of the human brain. How many times have you picked up your phone to send a text, and then ten minutes later found yourself scrolling through Instagram? That happens because of how your phone was designed. At casinos, slot machines are the most addicting games, and that's exactly why every social media platform from Facebook to TikTok to Twitter to LinkedIn uses the scroll feature.

I recognize that our phones help us do lots of daily functions—from managing our daily calendars and appointments to keeping us in touch with people through phone, text, and email. But the goal is to use our phones for the things we need and not get sucked into endless scrolling. The way you do this is simple: put your phone in another room or hide it away in a drawer. Keep it out of sight, and don't check it for a certain amount of time. If you do that, you'll be shocked how much easier it is to focus. I have a special drawer in my kitchen where I keep my phone. So if I need to send a text message, I must get up, go into the kitchen, open the drawer, and send the text. Once I do that, I make it a point to put the phone back in the drawer as quickly as possible and return to what I was doing. That tiny bit of resistance of having to stand up and walk to get my phone is all it takes to prevent me from feeling the need to constantly check it throughout the day. The goal is to become a person who uses their phone, not one whose phone uses them.

This is an example of a great way that you can start small. The first few times you put your phone away, it's going to feel strange, perhaps even like you're missing something. Boredom might creep in. That's okay. It's normal, and it's good to acknowledge the discomfort. For the first week, practice putting it away for thirty minutes or an hour at a time. Once you start to realize you can go without it and still function (probably even function better!), you can gradually build up to a longer schedule.

If you don't need your phone for work, maybe come up with a plan to put your phone away at 9 a.m. and don't allow yourself to touch it until noon. Then check all your messages, and when you're done, put it back and don't touch it again until 5 p.m.

A helpful widget on my phone called Screen Time tells me how long I spend on the phone over the course of a day or week. I've moved it to my home screen so it's the very first thing I see when I pick up my phone. Remember, we need to be aware of what is distracting us. Screen Time keeps me aware and helps me keep tabs on how often I'm looking at my phone. Every Sunday, I get a notification that tells me whether I looked at my phone that week more or less than the week before. It's become a game I play with myself as I try to get that screen time down as much as possible.

Look at the five apps you use the most on your phone and ask yourself whether the time you spend on those apps is helping you or hurting your efforts to get where you want to go in life. If you find one standing in your way at all, try deleting that app for thirty days to see how your life changes. After those thirty days, you can decide whether or not you want to reinstall it. If you do reinstall it, set some boundaries for yourself and get clear about how you're going to manage the time you spend on your phone. Ask yourself what you can do right now to free yourself from the distractions your phone creates.

Micro-action step: Put your phone in a drawer or another room for a set period of time. Try starting with thirty minutes and make a point to do this at least once a day for a week.

Notifications

Even if your phone is locked away in a drawer most of the day, you can still get distracted by all the notifications.

The first step is to become aware of which notifications you receive. Some are necessary—a text message from your sister, an alert about a doctor's appointment—but again, our phones are designed to keep us engaged, which means almost every app is set up to ping us about every little thing. If you are intentional about which notifications to keep on and which to turn off, you will be less distracted by messages and alerts you don't even care about.

Next, see how many notifications you can turn off. Start by turning off all your social media and news feed notifications. When in doubt, keep only the notifications that are beneficial to your life and help you get where you want to go. I no longer allow even text message notifications on my phone—nothing pops up or dings when there's a new message. The only way I know that a text has come in is when I intentionally open the messaging app. I do the same thing with email: I must open the app to see whether I have received any new messages. This puts me in charge of my phone, and therefore my time, instead of reacting to the demands of my phone. If I have blocked off 9 to 10 a.m. to spend time checking and responding to emails, I'm not tempted to check at 8:30 a.m. because I see that ten emails are waiting for me.

And don't forget about your computer. When I was writing this book at an Airbnb in Sedona, Arizona, I worked outside with my laptop with the Wi-Fi turned off because I didn't need Wi-Fi to use Microsoft Word. With the internet come the notifications that distract me from the work I need to do. I also do this when creating podcast episodes. I work on Word and disconnect my Wi-Fi for ninety minutes at a time to make sure I can focus my attention on the task at hand for that set period.

I realize that not everyone has the luxury of being able to go offline whenever they want. If you need access to your email throughout your workday (I know that some people expect, and need, quick responses), I recommend turning off the email notifications so that you can focus on deep work and click over to check emails when needed. Even when I was working on this book, I still needed to run my business, so I made sure to set aside time to plug back in and take care of anything that I needed to address.

When it comes to the internet, even if it's not actively alerting me to something, I know how easy it is to go down an internet rabbit hole and get distracted from the work I need to be doing. If possible, keep open only those programs you need to do your work, and shut down everything else. If you work on your computer often and find yourself getting distracted by the internet, look into a program like Freedom that blocks websites and apps to help you focus on the task at hand. Programs like these help take away the temptation to go down that internet rabbit hole, which also means you won't have to exert willpower to resist. Everyone's job and situation are different, so you have to find a system that works best for you.

The more distractions you can remove, the easier it will be for you to focus on what you're trying to do. And, you'll find that when you're focused on your task, it's easy to forget about the texts and emails that would otherwise grab your attention.

Micro-action step: Go to your phone's notification settings and disable any that you don't need immediately.

Other People

The people in our lives—our family members, our colleagues, our friends—are important and worth making time for. However, they can also draw our attention away from other things that are important.

Everyone's situation is different, but if you know that you need to sit down and get two hours of solid, focused work done, do you have a place where you can do that without being distracted by other people? If not, think of ways you can make it obvious to others that you're busy working, so they don't bother you. Sometimes it's as easy as putting on headphones to signal that you prefer not to be disturbed.

If you're in an office, you can close the door and put up a friendly sign that asks people not to distract you unless it's an emergency. If you're working at home and have kids, try to find a friend or family member who can watch them for a couple of hours. Hire a babysitter if necessary so you can go into a quiet space and do what you need to do to move the needle. Put a sign on the door also at home when you don't want to be distracted, asking your spouse or roommates not to enter or disturb you for the next few hours. Try to design a system that prevents other people from distracting you when you need to get focused work done.

Of course, I understand this can be complicated if you have family obligations. People often say that they can't set aside the necessary time to focus during the day because of their responsibilities to their family. I often hear "I can't because I have kids." But your kids shouldn't be the excuse for why you don't have the life you want; they should be the excuse for why you want to create that life—*for* your kids. They should be your "why." Stop using your kids as scapegoats and look inside yourself. Remember that if something is important to you, you will find a way; if something is not important, you will find an excuse.

> If something is important to you,
> you will find a way; if something is not
> important, you will find an excuse.

Instead of thinking of your family obligations as roadblocks, make your family members allies. Work with them. Talk to your partner about helping you carve out some time each day or week. Maybe your partner can do some of your chores. Just remember that every relationship is a two-way street, so try offering up something in return. If your partner is doing more than their fair share of housekeeping or child-rearing, offer to help in those areas so they can have more time for themselves. Then you can more easily carve out time for yourself without seeming selfish or demanding. Besides, helping your partner to refocus their life on what's most important for them will help keep you both accountable. True partners work together.

If this isn't an option for you, other ideas include those mentioned above: hire a babysitter or nanny if you have the means, or if money is tight, ask a friend or family member whether they can help out. Or, if that is off the table as well, look at your schedule and see whether you can squeeze in some work time before the kids get up or after they go to bed. Remember: small actions taken consistently over time add up to big changes.

Micro-action step: Identify people who might be a distraction to you while you try to get work done and design a system that lets you get time alone without neglecting any necessary obligations. If this is difficult, start small by setting aside thirty minutes, and continue to refine your system until you find one that works for you.

Physical Environment

The most productive people are not the ones with the most will-power, but the ones who designed their environment such that they don't have to test their willpower. I know I don't have the strongest willpower all the time, so by designing my environment in a way in which I won't be easily tempted by distraction, I'm setting myself up for success. Businessman and author W. Clement Stone said, "You are a product of your environment. So choose the environment that will best develop you toward your objective." How is your environment working for you or against you when it comes to distraction? When designing your own environment, ask yourself two questions:

1. How can I design my environment so that it is easier for me to take action?

2. How can I design my environment so that it is harder to distract myself from taking action?

Start by looking over the spaces you regularly spend time in and see what type of action they encourage. Whether you realize it or not, you have designed every room in your house to be suited toward some type of action or inaction. For example, in 99 percent of the living rooms I've walked into, all the couches and chairs face the television. Those rooms were designed for watching TV. That's the function of those spaces, and if that's how you want to spend your time in them, that's fine.

For some people, though, they are trying to get other things done in those rooms and find it hard not to turn on the TV. Americans are big TV watchers: in 2019, Netflix users spent an average of 2 hours every day watching Netflix, and Nielsen predicted that number increased to 3.2 hours during the coronavirus quarantine of 2020.[6] That's two to three hours every day that they could have used to work toward their goals.

If you're having trouble cutting out streaming services or cable, and you're spending a large portion of your time in a room that is designed for watching TV, you're setting yourself up for failure. If you want to spend your time in the living room reading instead of watching television, design the environment accordingly. Move the TV to another room and place books and magazines on any coffee table or end tables in the living room. What action would that encourage? You can't watch TV if it's not in the room, and chances are good you'll read a lot more because you designed the room according to what you want to accomplish.

This same principle applies to every environment where you spend time throughout the day, whether it's a bedroom, office, cubicle, or even your car. Design your environment to make it easier for you to take the action needed to accomplish your goals and harder for you to be distracted. For a long time, I was making an effort to not sit so much throughout the day, so instead of getting distracted by going outside for a walk and in an effort to design my work environment to support both work and exercise, I bought a treadmill and a computer stand so I could walk for an extra ninety minutes a day while working.

How can you design your environment to your advantage? For instance, what does your office setup look like? Whether that's an office outside of your home or in your home, think about what's working and what's not. How do you find yourself getting the most distracted, and what can you do to address this?

For instance, clutter can be distracting. I encourage you to keep your workspace clean. The fewer items on your desk, the fewer potential distractions. I keep my desk clear except for a laptop, external monitor, noise-canceling headphones, and a pen and paper. When I sit down there, I'm telling myself, and I can *see*, that it's time to focus and take action. You want to give yourself no choice but to get your work done.

> You want to give yourself no choice
> but to get your work done.

When many more people started to work from home during the coronavirus pandemic, people told me they got easily distracted, especially in the morning. When it was time to sit down and work at their desk, it was easier (and more fun) to sit on the couch instead and scroll through Instagram. If this sounds like you, let me suggest something that seems a little strange, but it works: take all the cushions off the couch and put them in a closet, so you aren't pulled in by the comfort of the couch. This way, you have no choice but to sit down at the desk and get to work. I'm serious. Have you ever tried to sit on a couch that doesn't have cushions? It's not very comfortable, so make it uncomfortable to distract yourself. After you build the new habit of working at your desk, you can put the cushions back.

Moving things off your desk and removing cushions from your couch are simple things, and that's the point. People assume that changes must be difficult and will require struggle to get them done, but we struggle only because we've mastered the art of distraction. It's all about making things as simple and easy as possible to remove the distractions that inhibit action.

Setting up your environment for success applies to other areas of your life besides work, too. Let's say that you want to get up early and go for a run. Getting up early isn't always easy, and even less so if you don't enjoy running! So try setting out your running clothes and everything you need before you go to bed so that your bleary, half-awake self the next morning doesn't have to put in additional work and can more easily get ready. If you need coffee in the morning before you leave, get a coffee maker with a timer so it will make coffee when your alarm goes off and a cup will be waiting for you by the time you get to the kitchen. If you take a water bottle with you when you run, fill it up and leave it in the fridge the night before, ready to go. It still might be difficult to get in the habit of running every morning, but if you design your environment the night before to remove possible resistance and make it harder to get distracted, you're making it easier for yourself and setting yourself up for success.

If you want to eat healthier food, start by removing all the snacks and junk food from your house. Go through your fridge and pantry and get rid of every food that's not going to help you achieve your goal. When you go to the store, don't buy that food because it only leads to temptation. Trust me, I know. I love sweets and sugar, so I know not to keep any of that in my house because my willpower is weak. I can't have just a little bit of sugar or only a few Skittles; I tend to eat the entire bag, no matter how big it is. My discipline in a room with Skittles is completely different (or nonexistent) from my discipline in a room without Skittles. I deal with that by removing the distraction and creating an environment that keeps me on the path where I want to go.

Meal prepping is another great way to remove distractions and stay focused on eating healthy foods. Every Sunday night, prep all your meals for the week ahead. This way, you make all your decisions for the entire week at once, instead of taking the mental energy to make a new decision every night. Your discipline changes as your environment changes, and most disciplined people have become that way because they have removed distractions and temptations from the environments where they spend their time.

Whether it's a living space, an office, a desk, or a kitchen, the environment of people who are successful looks different from the environment of people who are not successful. It's not that successful people are more disciplined; it's that they have removed everything that will make it harder for them to be disciplined. Set up your environment so it's easier to become successful. It's really not difficult; it just requires your being more intentional about your space and making it optimal for the type of action you need to take.

Micro-action step: Spend ten minutes looking at the spaces where you regularly work and spend time and ask yourself what type of actions those spaces encourage. If those actions don't line up with your goals, try to make modifications to those environments that would help you be more productive.

Social Environment

The expectations of the group of people you spend the most time with will dictate the actions you take or don't take. One way to significantly change your life is to start hanging out with people whose normal actions line up with the desired action you want to take. You want to stop drinking alcohol? Hang out with people who don't drink. Want to build a successful business? Hang out with people who either already have a successful business or are working to build those businesses. Want a great marriage? Hang out with people who have great marriages and make that a priority. Want to be a great parent? Hang out with exceptional parents of great kids.

When I was twenty-four, I moved into a house with Reggie, a bodybuilder. This was a time when I was skinny and struggled to put on any muscle, no matter how often I worked out. This guy was massive and constantly talked about working out and how to eat right. And he was always trying to learn more from his bodybuilding friends. He was in love with bodybuilding, and as my roommate, he was the person I spent the most time with in my social circle. We were around each other all the time, so not only did I start working out more and eating better, but I started changing the way I did everything related to my body. Pretty soon, I was in the best shape of my life. I lived with Reggie for only six months, but during that time I gained seventeen pounds of muscle.

This can work both ways. Two years later, I moved to Austin and into a house with a friend who had already been in the city for a couple of years, so he had established his own social circle. As soon as I moved in, his social circle became my social circle. And this was a group of people who partied a lot. Every night of the week, it was easy to find someone who was going out. It was fun and they were my friends, so I probably ended up drinking three or four times a week. That was normal. I also knew that it was holding me back from growing personally and professionally, so I intentionally started to move away from that lifestyle.

At twenty-nine, I started my company and began networking with other entrepreneurs. Eventually, I spent more time with them than I did with my old group of friends. I still liked my old friends, but my social circle changed. I then met someone at an event in Orlando who ran a business that was making about $4 million a year. I wanted to build a business like his, so he became a mentor in addition to being a close friend. He was also a recovering alcoholic, and most of the people I met through him rarely drank, so I drank much less. I realized how much more productive I was when I wasn't drinking. I noticed that having a few drinks on Sunday night could slow me down until Wednesday, which meant I was operating at 100 percent only Thursday and Friday. So in a few years, I went from partying like crazy to drinking maybe once or twice a month. It wasn't that I made a concerted effort to stop drinking, but my social circle changed from people who often drank to people who did not. Many factors go into how the body metabolizes alcohol, but most people are shocked to learn that alcohol can stay in your system for up to eighty hours.[7] As soon as I cut down on alcohol, I realized how much it had been holding me back, and that made me want to cut down even more.

The other big change was that I went from hanging out with people who had jobs to hanging out with entrepreneurs who were their own bosses. The idea of owning my business no longer seemed like a weird thing but a normal thing. In my new social environment with people who had different priorities, we talked about our struggles and successes, and we all helped each other out. Fast-forward seven years, and now my five closest friends are all running successful businesses. There was some intention to it, but it mostly happened naturally because I gravitated toward people who were doing something similar or had already achieved what I wanted.

Your social circle isn't restricted by proximity. A few years ago, I went to an event for coaches in a similar industry to mine and met three people—two from California and one from Canada—with whom I got along well and started doing monthly Zoom calls to brainstorm ideas. Since we started doing that, we all became closer and everyone's business has experienced a lot of growth. We all thrived because of the social environment we designed. I believe so much in going to events, attending conferences, joining masterminds, and learning from other people from all over who are interested in the same things you are interested in. As Tony Robbins says, "Proximity is power."

You've probably heard the saying that you are the average of the five people you spend the most time with, and it's true. Look at your five closest friends and I'll bet you make around the same amount of money, are in the same shape, drink the same amount of alcohol, and have the same general approach to career, family, and business. We can't help but become the people we spend our time with. I'm not saying that you have to get rid of people in your life who aren't on the same path, but you can choose to spend more time with those who are on the same trajectory. Give yourself enough time, and your actions will match the expectations of those people you spend the most time with.

Micro-action step: Identify a person or a group of people who have goals similar to yours and with whom you want to build a closer relationship. Reach out to them via email or text this week.

*   *   *

The problem is not that you don't have enough time. Everyone gets the same twenty-four hours every day. That will never change, but you can change how well you utilize that time by actively removing distractions and temptations. That makes all the difference. Our technologies—smartphones, tablets, computers, televisions—are amazing, but if you're not careful, they can become time-sucking distractions. You want technology to be a tool, not your master.

Start paying closer attention to what you spend your time doing. Once you can become more aware of what's distracting you from what you need to accomplish, you can adjust and put systems in place to get back on track. Do that and it will feel like the universe has gifted you your life back in the form of a few extra hours every day.

Journal Prompts

- Write down everything that distracts you from taking action or gets in the way of doing what you need to do to get the life you want.

- Review that list and write down how you can remove as many of those distractions as possible when you need to focus and take action.

- How can you change and design your workspaces to eliminate distraction and encourage the action you want to take?

- Who are the five people you spend the most time with? How are they helping or hindering your progress?

- Think about your personal goals and then research conferences and networking events near you, or even just places where you think people who have similar goals would hang out. Consider how you can incorporate these activities into your schedule.

For more journal prompts and video lessons from this book, go to: https://RobDial.com/LevelUp.

CHAPTER 7

One Step at a Time

How to Get It All Done

I have a friend in the military who seems to get more done than anybody else I know. He's super productive, so one day I asked him: "How do you find the time to get everything done? Is it something they taught you in the military? What's the secret?"

He told me, "They teach us to live life on our front foot."

He explained how we live life either on our front foot or on our back foot. When we're on our front foot, we have forward motion. That's being proactive. That's leveling up. But when we're on our back foot, we're retreating. That's being reactive. It's the difference between being intentional and being unintentional. The most successful people are proactive and have a plan for what they're going to do every day, but too many people wake up and spend their day in reaction mode, while trying to put out fires.

When you lean forward on your front foot and take one step after the next to go those first hundred feet (remember Living in the Headlights in Chapter 5?), you build up momentum. And once you start to feel that momentum, it's essential to keep it going because stopping and then starting again takes a lot more effort. Momentum is one of the most underrated components of building the life you want, and yours should start the minute you wake up. Remember that motivation follows action, so if you remain consistent, you will generate momentum.

When a car stalls and you have to push it, the hardest part is getting the car moving; but once it gets rolling, it can almost get away from you because it's going so fast. If you let the car slow to a stop, you have to expend a lot of energy just to get it moving once again. That's why when you start to feel momentum each day, you want to ride it out: because it makes things so much easier than expending the energy required to constantly stop and start.

Start the Day with Small Wins

Little things have a big impact, and you can take several small actions immediately after waking up in the morning that will help you create momentum.

1. Never Hit Snooze

When your alarm goes off in the morning, what do you do? Are you the person who jumps out of bed, ready and excited to attack the day? Or do you hit the snooze button and roll back over? Trust me, I know how hard it is to get up. I love sleeping. I could sleep for thirteen hours straight if I didn't set my alarm in the morning. But if you hit that snooze button, you automatically start the day with a loss.

When you set your alarm the night before, you were fully conscious and you had a plan for the next day, and part of that plan was getting up at a certain time. When the alarm goes off, it's easy for the brain to persuade you to hit snooze because you aren't thinking of the consequences.

From now on, when your alarm goes off in the morning, instead of hitting snooze, get out of bed. That's your first win of the day.

I always encourage people to get a real alarm clock instead of using a phone alarm, which can lead to being distracted by the phone. Also, try moving your alarm to the other side of the room so you have to get out of bed to shut it off. It's much harder to hit snooze if you're already on your feet!

2. Make Your Bed

Once you're awake, the first thing I advise you to do is make your bed. It takes two minutes, maybe even less, but it creates a little bit more momentum and is another small win. Plus, it keeps you from getting back into bed. More significantly, you've gotten your first two wins of the day, and you haven't even been up for five minutes.

For the longest time, I didn't think it made sense for me to make my bed. I didn't spend any time in my bedroom. All I did was sleep there, so what was the point of making my bed if I was just going to sleep in the thing later anyway? But then I realized just how powerful that simple action can be. It created a small sense of accomplishment, and it took no time at all.

Admiral William H. McRaven's 2014 commencement speech at the University of Texas went viral and became the inspiration for his bestselling book *Make Your Bed: Little Things That Can Change*

Your Life . . . and Maybe the World. In it, he lays out this idea and other principles that he learned during Navy SEAL training that provided the foundation needed to overcome many of life's challenges. What do you have to lose? This one is a gimmie. Make your bed.

3. Complete Your Morning Routine

There's a ton of material out there on morning routines, but you don't need to come up with a huge checklist that will take up a big chunk of your morning. Just pick out a few things that you want to do that will jumpstart your day's momentum. The point is to be intentional so you're starting the day on your terms. You want to find a routine that fits your schedule and needs. For example, if you have kids, wake up thirty to sixty minutes before they do, so you can get what you need done at the beginning of the day.

In addition to the basics, such as showering and brushing your teeth, your morning routine might include

- Meditating

- Reading ten pages of a book

- Going for a jog

- Doing some yoga

- Journaling

- Sitting in silence

- Working out

You can do all these things, you can pick one or two, or you can come up with your own ideas.

If you've never had a morning routine before, or have had trouble keeping consistent with one, I suggest you start with two activities and add more as you get comfortable. Set aside a certain amount of time so you can get what you want done without feeling rushed. You don't want this to be a chore. It's meant to motivate you and leave you feeling accomplished, but it's also how you do things that fill you up in the morning. You'll feel much more in control of the rest of your day than if the alarm had simply started you on a frantic race to the door.

4. Make Your To-Do List

At the end of your morning routine, take ten minutes to visualize and plan out your day. We are going to do this by making a short to-do list. The operative word here: short.

Consider the Pareto Principle, also known as the 80/20 Rule. In this context, it means that 20 percent of the things you do daily will bring you 80 percent of the results you are looking for in life. On the flip side, 80 percent of the things you do every day will bring you only 20 percent of the results, so it's important to identify what those most productive actions are that will generate the results you're looking for. Smart businesspeople identify the top 20 percent of their revenue-generating activities and spend the majority of their days doing those things.

Some people come up with extremely long to-do lists that have dozens of items. I get it: there are so many things in our work and personal lives that we need to get done, the list can grow and grow. Many people even like to write down things they've already done and then cross them off because it makes them feel like they've accomplished something. But none of that helps. Why? Because so many of the items on that long list don't fall into that 20 percent category that will generate the most results. You might have to do laundry. It's easy, and it's something you can cross off your list, but is it helping you accomplish your goals? If it's 11 a.m. on a Tuesday and your priority is building your business, you shouldn't be doing laundry. Find another time to do it.

Don't get me wrong; the items on that long to-do list are still important. You have to do the dishes and laundry at some point, but when you have a long to-do list, you can easily feel so overwhelmed that you don't get anything accomplished.

From now on, every morning, single out the *three* most important needle-moving tasks. Next, take a three-by-five-inch index card and number the most important items on your list: one, two, three. Don't put this list anywhere on your phone because then you run the risk of being distracted by your phone every time you check the list. Instead, put this index card in your purse or pocket, so you take it with you everywhere you go.

The number one item on that list is nonnegotiable. Do not go to bed that night until you finish the first thing on the list. It is your priority for the day. That doesn't mean you need to do it first, but if you can get to it first, get it done. Sometimes that isn't possible, and you need to get other tasks done before you address that number one item; but you want to look over your schedule every morning and move things around on your calendar to make sure you get that first item on your list done. Imagine how much you would improve in just one year if you always completed the most important task you had to do every day.

Once you get number one done, number two becomes your priority and primary focus, and then number three; but even if you get only number one done, you've still made a tremendous amount of progress that day. You can get all those other little items from the long to-do list done later when it's not your productive work time. Or, if it helps put your mind at ease, schedule them into your calendar for a time when you know you can get to them, after the priorities are done.

As much of a struggle as it might be to get these things done, imagine how much easier it will be afterwards and the sense of accomplishment you'll feel. You'll thank yourself tomorrow, even as you put new things on your list.

5. Don't Look at Your Phone

Avoid looking at your phone for as long as possible in the morning because that will immediately turn your attention to thinking and worrying about all the text messages, emails, and tasks you need to do that day. Your momentum will be instantly diffused, and your priorities confused. Why do I know this? Because there is Rob before he looks at his phone and a Rob after. The creative part of my brain that wants to learn and grow is most powerful in the morning, but as soon as I look at my phone, that power begins to dwindle. If you can make it ten or thirty minutes without looking at your phone, that's great. Two hours? Even better. Another small win that adds up to big productivity.

* * *

These small wins are important because every win, no matter how tiny, releases a little bit of dopamine. And dopamine, as you'll learn in Part III, is the chemical of motivation. It's like you're knocking over dominoes, and once one goes, they all go.

It doesn't matter what you're trying to do, either. All you need are a bunch of small wins, each impelling the next. We often think of success as one huge event, when in reality, we don't notice the micro-actions that contributed to that larger result. Success involves doing the small things over and over every day, building momentum week after week, until you get to a point down the road where you arrive wherever it is you're trying to go.

Being Productive Versus Being Busy

The point of a to-do list with only three items is to narrow down the number of things you do daily. When you narrow your focus, you increase the quality of your output. You're not scattered or spreading yourself too thin, so your brain is all-in. This applies to almost everything you do in life, especially when looking to get the most important tasks done every day, but you must make sure that all three of those items are needle-moving activities. A lot of people trick themselves into thinking they're doing needle-moving activities when they're just being busy.

There is a difference between being productive and being busy. Let's say that you want to start training for a 5K, so you come up with an extensive workout and running routine. What you need to do is get out and go for a run. That's a productive activity, but that's not what a lot of people do when they set out to achieve that goal. They think they first need to get some running outfits and a new pair of running shoes, so they spend their time shopping for all the best gear. That stuff can be helpful, but what they really need to do is just run. All the other stuff is just tricking themselves into thinking they're being productive when they are really just being busy.

When I ran my first sales office, we used to do these things called phone jams where you try to make as many sales calls as possible. People would come into the office saying they wanted to make a hundred phone calls that day, but two hours later, they had made only six. When I'd ask them what they'd been doing, I'd hear answers like "I've been organizing my numbers" or "I've been reviewing my script." They were doing so many things other than making the actual calls, tricking themselves into inaction. They thought they were being productive, but really they were just acting busy and not being productive at all.

You need to focus on what you need to do to be productive and move the needle. With everything you do, ask yourself, "Is what I'm doing right now bringing me closer to my goal?" If not, stop. If so, go.

How Much Energy Do You Have?

If you want to take action and be productive, you need an alert mind. An alert mind comes down to energy, and that's influenced by four factors that you must monitor and stay on top of if you want to get things done: sleep, light, food, and water.

1. Sleep

Sleep plays a major role in your energy levels and is often the first issue that needs to be addressed. A 2018 study that assessed more than ten thousand people found that roughly half of them experienced a decline in cognitive performance when they slept less than seven to eight hours per night. Getting the right amount of sleep matters.[1]

If you want to have a productive day, it starts the night before. Try to sleep seven to eight hours a night and in a completely dark room. It's also worth investing in a comfortable bed if you don't have one. You will spend a third of your life sleeping on it. Investing in a good bed is one of the most important investments you will ever make.

2. Light

A 2017 study published in *Sleep Health* showed that exposure to morning sunlight resulted in greater alertness and overall sleep health among a group of office workers. It can also improve mood. People exposed to sunlight in the morning experienced less stress and lower levels of depression than those who were not exposed to sunlight.[2] That makes getting outside and soaking in a little bit of sunlight during that first hour after waking up so important.

Within the first hour you're awake, get in the habit of going outside, even for just a few minutes. Even if it's cloudy, your eyes will take in photons from the sun that help you become more alert and stop producing melatonin, which is the hormone that helps your body fall asleep. When I started doing this, I became much more alert, not just in the moment when exposed to sunlight, but throughout the day. That's why it's so important to get outside.

Even if you can't get outside, you can still get the benefits of certain kinds of light. There have been many studies of blue-enriched white light and how it might contribute to increased cognitive performance and help people feel less drowsy in the morning.[3] You can buy blue lights specifically made for this purpose, and even most all-white light bulbs have some blue light in them. If the sun isn't out, consider turning on all of the lights so your space is illuminated.

3. Food

It's not the tryptophan in turkey on Thanksgiving that makes you want to take a nap as much as it is all the food you ate. Between about 15 and 30 percent of your daily energy is devoted to digestion.[4]

If you take a mental note of how you feel after eating, you'll start to notice how some foods deplete your energy, especially if you eat too much. So eat foods early in the day that give you energy and those later in the day that deplete it. Everyone is different. Some people need to eat breakfast in the morning, and others find they have more energy when they fast in the morning. I fall into the second category and typically don't eat anything until one or two o'clock in the afternoon. It took me a while to reach that understanding, and I don't do it every day. I pay attention to what my body needs. If I'm hungry in the morning, I'll snack on fruit, and if I do eat a meal, I'll make some eggs. I'll eat my heartier meals later in the day, when I'm done working out, so I will have more energy to focus and be productive.

What's most important is that you are intentional about the food you eat. Energy levels are an incredibly important part of taking action, so I've learned to plan what I eat around my working schedule to ensure that I will be productive throughout the day.

It may sound counterintuitive, but when it comes time to focus, don't underestimate the power of a little bit of hunger. Studies show that intermittent fasting can improve brain function.[5] You don't want to starve yourself, or have your blood sugar level drop too low, but hunger increases your release of adrenaline. There's something instinctual about it because thousands of years ago, humans had to focus on when they went out to hunt and find food. So being hungry can be an important part of getting more focused every day. Everyone's body is different, so try it out for a week to see whether and how hunger affects your energy levels.

4. Water

We lose anywhere between sixteen and thirty-two ounces of water every night simply by breathing. Most of us are dehydrated when we wake up in the morning, and dehydration can affect cognitive function and alertness.[6] So it's important to stay hydrated. How much water you need to drink depends on many factors, but as soon as you get up and make your bed, try getting in the habit of drinking one or two glasses of water right away to rehydrate yourself. You can even make this part of your routine, so it's another small win that gives you momentum at the beginning of the day.

The one thing you don't want to drink first thing in the morning is coffee. Some people can't imagine not drinking that first cup right away, but stick with me here because studies show that cortisol, your stress hormone, is elevated forty-five minutes after waking up.[7] That means it's in your best interest to avoid caffeine at the start of the day. You might sometimes find yourself flooded with anxiety and stressful thoughts first thing in the morning. Coffee will both further dehydrate you and increase your cortisol levels, creating more anxiety and stress. Drink water instead. It rehydrates your body, improves brain function, and gives you more energy. Wait an hour before you have your first cup of coffee. This will help you be much more productive in the morning, and you'll feel better, too.

The downside of coffee is that it provides an initial spike of energy, but then that spike disappears, leaving you feeling like you need more coffee. Some people prefer drinking tea made from the yerba mate plant instead of coffee because, even though it contains caffeine, they don't experience the same crash as they do with coffee. It's also hydrating and may have numerous health benefits, including stimulating the production of GLP-1, which can help regulate appetite so you don't feel as hungry throughout the day.[8]

Energy Planning

Everyone feels different at different times of the day. Some people are more productive in the morning and others are night owls. I have a good friend who gets most of his work done late at night. Not everyone likes to stay up that late, but it works for him.

A good way to figure out when your energy levels are at their highest and therefore when you are likely to be your most productive is a simple process that I call energy tracking. It's exactly what it sounds like. Set your alarm for every single hour that you are awake, and when it goes off, make a note of your energy levels for the previous hour on a scale of one to ten—one being no energy and ten being the most. If you do this over a few days, you'll notice some patterns and how your energy levels tend to be consistent from day to day. You can take advantage of this by completing your most important, needle-moving activities during those time periods when you feel the most focused and your energy levels are at their highest.

Energy planning has become essential for me to get done everything I need to do each day. Because I own two companies, put out three to four podcast episodes a week, and offer self-development courses through the Mindset Mentor, I have clients, employees, and listeners who are all relying on me. I have to know when my energy will be high because that's when I need to get my needle-moving tasks done.

I know some of you have children and others work in an office, so your energy plan will be very different from mine, but seeing how I organize my day around my energy levels can be a helpful example.

- I typically wake up at 6:30 a.m., when the alarm first goes off, and make my bed.

- I meditate with my wife for twenty minutes, followed by reading or journaling.

- After I visualize my day and make my three-item to-do list, I journal the answer to one question: "What can I do to make today amazing?" I ask and answer that question every single day because that helps me be intentional. Sometimes what makes my day amazing is getting done the first item of my to-do list. Or it could be playing pickleball with friends when I'm done working because sometimes making the day amazing means doing something fun.

- At 7:30 a.m., I usually make some coffee and spend time with my wife and our dogs. We've become very intentional about spending an hour together before our days get super busy.

- 8:30 to 9:15 a.m. is my creative time, when I make social media content and come up with ideas for the *Mindset Mentor* podcast. My team knows that I will not answer any calls or texts during this time.

- 9:15 a.m. is when I finally check for emails and texts on my phone (which has been in a drawer), three hours after I wake up. I answer any that I need to address, and then I disconnect again, putting the phone back in a drawer.

- From 9:30 to 10:30 a.m. I work out. This is the period of the day when I have the most physical energy. Some people have more energy for physical activity later in the day, but this works best for me. By 10:30 a.m. I feel empowered.

- 10:30 a.m. to 2:30 p.m. is when I get my focused work done because this is my high-energy time of the day. These four hours are my sacred time. Once again, I don't answer any emails or texts during this time because I spend it knocking out my most important tasks, as well as the number one to-do item on the index card in my back pocket. If it doesn't take long, I can also do items two and three, but some days that first item might take a couple of hours, so that is what I prioritize.

- 2:30 p.m. is when I typically have my first meal of the day, and then until 6:00 p.m. I do all the ancillary things I need to get done that don't require my most intense focus, such as making Zoom calls and checking in with my team. My energy is not as high during this period, so I make sure that I've already taken care of all my priorities.

- 6:00 p.m. is my nonnegotiable turn-off time. Yes, there are days when I have to work a little bit later, but 95 percent of the time I'm done at 6:00 p.m., and I completely shut off. When I'm done, I'm done.

- 7:30 p.m. is when I have dinner, and I typically won't eat again until 2:30 p.m. the following day. My energy level is decreasing, so I usually spend the time until 9:30 hanging out with my wife and friends or reading.

- 9:30 p.m. is when I start to get ready for bed.

- By 10:00 p.m. I make sure I've written down my goals for the next day and anything I want to improve upon. I believe this is important because it allows these thoughts to seep through my subconscious as I fall asleep.

- 10:30 p.m. at the latest is lights out, which allows me to get eight hours of sleep.

The Importance of Logging Off

People often overlook the importance of having a specific time when they stop doing work. When I first started my business, I didn't take any days off and worked from 8 a.m. to 11 p.m. every day, sometimes even later. Most nights I didn't go to bed until 1 a.m., and then I'd get up the next day and do it all over because I thought that I didn't deserve time off until I got to where I wanted to be in life.

Have you ever felt that way? It's very common, but it turns out to be a trap. People like to set big goals, and then when they get close to achieving them, they push them further out and think of bigger and bigger goals. Many people's goals are like the horizon, which you can never catch.

Everything changed for me years ago when I read a book titled *The ONE Thing: The Surprisingly Simple Truth Behind Extraordinary Results* by Gary Keller, who owns one of the biggest real estate companies in the world. He wrote about the importance of scheduling free time. At first, I resisted, but then I figured that this guy was a billionaire, so maybe I should listen to him because he probably knew something that I didn't. He suggested thinking of scheduling time like working out: when you work a muscle really hard, it needs to rest before it can grow, and the same is true for your brain. If you constantly overwork your brain, you will burn out, lose focus, and your productivity will decrease. It feels counterintuitive, but it's true. Taking breaks from work will actually help you work better. Take weekends off, and you'll start to realize that you come back on Monday feeling refreshed and you can be more productive.

You're also more productive during the time before a break because of the pressure leading up to that cutoff time. Think about how productive you are the day before you go away on vacation. When are you the best at studying? The night before an exam. When do you do your best work? The night before a project is due. Your brain works better with a cutoff time because there are no other options.

This concept was mind-boggling to me at first because I didn't see how I could accomplish more by working less. But what I learned was that I was utilizing my time better. Since I know that my levels of focus and energy are usually lower by 6 p.m., I made that my cutoff time. I start doing my final sweep of all the tasks that are not a high priority about an hour or two before. At the end of the day, I write down everything I need to do the next day. This way, I don't have to worry about forgetting anything, so my brain can release it instead of worrying about it that evening. Then, I disconnect and get ready to come back the next day and be highly productive.

> You don't want to spend so much time trying
> to make a living that you forget to make
> a life. Have some fun. Enjoy your life.

You don't want to spend so much time trying to make a living that you forget to make a life. Have some fun. Enjoy your life. When you do that, you will be even more productive when you sit down and focus to get work done.

* * *

Momentum is built through the simplest of tasks. All it requires is a little bit of planning and self-awareness to make sure the actions you're taking are moving you in the right direction and closer to your goals. Instead of fighting an uphill battle, make things easier for yourself by racking up small wins first thing in the morning, boiling your to-do list down to three essential needle-moving tasks, and knocking those out during times of the day when you have the most energy. These aren't big changes. It's an easy strategy that requires a slight mindset shift in the way you approach your day. That will lay the groundwork and better prepare you to do the more focused work that requires your undivided attention.

Journal Prompts

- Before going to bed tonight, jot down what you did today. Be honest with yourself about how you spent your time.

- In what ways do you tend to trick yourself into thinking you're productive when you're really just being busy?

- How can you rearrange your schedule to make sure you're doing your most important needle-moving activities at times when you have the most energy?

For more journal prompts and video lessons from this book, go to: https://RobDial.com/LevelUp.

CHAPTER 8

Focus

The Secret to Productivity

Rory McIlroy's 2011 meltdown at the Masters (see Chapter 6) didn't end his career. Like any great athlete, he learned to adjust and bounced back. That led to changes both on the course and off.

Years later, McIlroy spoke about how he changed his off-the-course routine during tournaments to help him focus. Today, he doesn't watch any golf or listen to any media coverage of the event he's participating in because he knows it could negatively affect his mindset and become a distraction. He shuts himself off from the outside world, which includes restrictions on his phone and social media use because they both distract him. He still watches movies or TV at night to decompress, but he's found a way to eliminate the distractions that cause him to lose focus during a tournament. As he's gone on to win four major tournaments since his meltdown, the results speak for themselves.

The definition of focused attention, the simplest form of attention, is "the ability to respond discretely to specific visual, auditory or tactile stimuli." Sustained attention is "the ability to maintain a consistent behavioral response during continuous and repetitive activity."[1] The more focused you are, the more brainpower you bring to that action; the less focused, the less brainpower you bring. With more focus you get more output for each minute of input, but most people struggle to focus on the task at hand. Why would you want to bring anything less than 100 percent of your brainpower to anything you do? Focus is the secret to productivity, and the more productive you are, the more you can move the needle with each action you take.

Focus and concentration are skills that you can hone and improve. It's not like some people are born with focus and some people aren't. Everyone can get better at it, but we've been training ourselves to be distracted for so long that the mental muscles required to focus might be weak. That's why you must be diligent in your efforts. So much of this process comes down to learning how to become more intentional and proactive, and how to start each day leaning forward on your front foot instead of being on your back foot in reaction mode. When you do that, you start to create the shift in mindset necessary to focus and get things done. You then realize that saying "yes" to something means saying "no" to something else. So, if you say "yes" to answering a text from a friend when you're trying to take focused action and get other work done, in that moment you're saying the text is more important than the work you're trying to do. If you're scrolling through Instagram when your energy levels are at their highest, in that moment you're saying Instagram is more important than your needle-moving activities.

Focus and distraction are two sides of the same coin. The more you work to improve the former, the less distracted you will be. Yes, your mind will still wander—your brain also wants to distract you— but the more you work on focusing, the easier it will be to pull yourself back to the task that needs your attention. Similar to mindfulness meditation training, that act of recognizing the distraction, not giving in, and refocusing will strengthen that muscle and allow you to go deeper.[2] Do that repeatedly and you will soon discover that you don't get distracted as easily.

Doing this is not impossible and doesn't require willpower. Here I present seven tools I've researched and tried myself that will make this process easier. Some may work better than others, but through trial and error you can find a system that fits your needs. With the help of these tools—the Pomodoro Technique, visual focus, lighting, sound, an accountability partner, movement, and cold water (really!)—your focus will feel superhuman compared with the way it feels now. Talk about leveling up!

The Pomodoro Technique

The Pomodoro Technique helps you manage your time with a simple timer: You set a timer and work for twenty-five minutes on one task and only that one task. You can't do anything else. When those twenty-five minutes are up, you take a five-minute break, and then do another twenty-five-minute session followed by a five-minute break. If you do four sessions, that's one hundred minutes of hard work that you got done.

According to a 2016 study of about two thousand office workers in the United Kingdom, the average worker gets less than three hours of work done during an eight-hour day.[3] With the Pomodoro Technique, you can get twice as much work done in a single day. Think of how much further ahead of the competition you will be if you do this for an entire year. That's the power of learning how to get focused work done. Here's how the Pomodoro Technique works:

- First, remove all distractions. Put your phone away and use noise-canceling headphones if necessary to help block out the outside world. I like to keep a cup of coffee, tea, or yerba mate next to me, so I can stay alert.

- Then, clear your mind by doing a brain dump before you begin. That means using a pen and paper to write down all the things floating around in your head so you can release them. It doesn't matter if they are big or small; write them all down. This way, you won't be worried about forgetting anything, and you'll know you can attend to whatever you need to do after the session, but it won't be on your mind when you're trying to focus. Keep that notebook handy during all of your work sessions to jot down any more ideas that come to mind, so they won't pull away your focus or steal time away from what you're trying to do. And you will have ideas; just make sure to flip the page of the notebook after you've jotted down your notes so your notes don't distract you. You're basically closing out all the tabs you have open in your brain. This will give you more bandwidth to focus on your task.

- When it's time to start work, set your timer for twenty-five minutes. It's important not to use the timer on your phone because that can be a big distraction. At first, it can be a struggle to hit the twenty-five-minute mark without being distracted, but the more you practice and push through, the more focused you become. Even though your mental muscles may be weak right now, you will build them up and your ability to focus will become stronger as you practice. Eventually, you can build up to thirty minutes, and then thirty-five. Many people do something I call Pomodoro Plus where they work for forty-five minutes and then take ten minutes off. But please, start with twenty-five minutes on and five minutes off until your focus muscles become stronger.

- Set the timer for your five-minute break. This break is extremely important; don't look at your phone or do anything else during it. Instead, try to go outside and let your mind wander. Stare off into the distance. Look at the horizon or skyline; maybe go for a walk. As we learned earlier, sunlight can help with your alertness, so go outside if possible. What's happening when you take a break is called hippocampal replay.[4] The hippocampus, the same part of the brain that stores all your memories when you sleep, will replay the last action you did. And it does so about ten times faster than when you first completed the action. It's storing away that information, which is why the Pomodoro Technique can be so effective when you're studying or trying to learn something new, such as an instrument. After five minutes, come back for another twenty-five-minute session of intense focus.

I know some people will immediately say, "I don't have a desk job; this won't work for me," or "My job requires me to be on my phone, so I can't put it away." One common example is Realtors. My mom has been a Realtor for my entire life. My sister and brother-in-law are also Realtors, as are two of my closest friends. One of them used to drive me crazy because he was always on his phone. Yes, he would scroll through listings and field calls all day long, but he also needed to write offers, post listings, and do everyday administrative work. If you're a Realtor or have a similar job, doing one or two twenty-five-minute sessions of the Pomodoro Technique to knock out those tasks can significantly increase your productivity and help you work more efficiently. And if you find that you can't disconnect from your phone for an hour or half hour, you can look for other ways to set boundaries and come up with a system to unplug so you can do focused work.

The reason the Pomodoro Technique works so well is because it requires single-tasking, not multitasking. You may think that you're a good multitasker, but I promise you, you aren't. Nobody is. It's impossible. Multitasking divides your attention, which isn't a big deal if you're listening to a podcast and making a sandwich, but if you're trying to focus on work or complete something complex, multitasking will divide your focus, and you end up doing something called task-switching instead. As the brain switches between tasks, it has to slow down, so it misses information and makes mistakes as it attempts to reconfigure and complete the next task.[5]

Multiple studies have found that the more people multitask, the *less* they accomplish. In an article in *Harvard Business Review*, professor of psychology Paul Atchley wrote, "Based on over a half-century of cognitive science and more recent studies on multitasking, we know that multitaskers do less and miss information. It takes time (an average of 15 minutes) to re-orient to a primary task after a distraction, such as an email. Efficiency can drop by as much as 40%. Long-term memory suffers and creativity—a skill associated with keeping in mind multiple, less common, associations—is reduced."[6]

This isn't an isolated finding. Study after study show that multitasking lowers the quality of production, so just don't do it. Focus on one thing, and one thing only. Bring your complete attention to each task. You'll get it done faster, and it will be of higher quality. Bring 100 percent of your brainpower and focus to every action.

It might take time before you can focus for a full twenty-five minutes, but just like putting time in at the gym, you will see improvement and results if you stick to it. In his book *Deep Work: Rules for Focused Success in a Distracted World*, Cal Newport writes about "deliberate practice," which is "the systematic stretching of your ability for a given skill."[7] This is how you can expand your focus, but go easy on yourself if you struggle on some days. Although on good days I can focus for forty-five minutes, some days I can barely reach that twenty-five-minute mark. Still, I make sure to push myself to complete at least those twenty-five minutes every single time.

Don't be alarmed if you feel resistance at first. Everyone feels resistance when they try to focus on something new. That's why there is no such thing as writer's block; at least not the way that most people think of it. It's not a creativity block; it's your brain resisting a new action. Your brain wants to stay on its back foot because that's most energy efficient, so you must get it on its front foot to focus. Fortunately, just as the solution to starting the day right is to give yourself some small wins, the way to break the block is to simply write. Write anything! It could be something like "Today is Tuesday and I am wearing a black shirt. For breakfast I ate eggs." Write whatever comes to mind. All you're doing is warming up your brain just like you would warm up your body before lifting weights at the gym. Those first six minutes will be difficult, so you must fight to stay on task. After you do this once, it will be easier to do the next time and so on.

When getting started, find a pattern that works for you, but it's important that you block out that specific period for focused work and be dedicated and consistent. When you turn this act into a ritual or habit, it helps your brain get used to it, and that will cut down on future resistance and give you less reason to avoid acting.

Visual Focus

You can utilize the *way* you look at your workspace to help you focus better by locking in on a small visual field directly in front of you. The density of the receptors in our eyes is higher in the center of our visual field than it is on the sides, which is why the center image is clear, while what's off to the side is blurrier. Visual clarity is more conducive to attention and mental focus.

If you know that you need to focus on work that you're doing on your computer, or you're about to start a session of the Pomodoro Technique, concentrate on your visual focus first. That means focusing visually on something right in front of you, staring at it for about two minutes. You want to block out your peripheral vision, restrict your visual window, and blink as little as possible. It might take a little while before you can visually focus, but you will start to feel your brain warm up. What's happening is something called vergence eye movement that activates neurons that trigger epinephrine (adrenaline in your brain) and acetylcholine, which are associated with visual focus. And once you focus your eyes, your mind will follow.[8]

Before I started writing today, I focused visually on my computer and took it a step further by putting on a hat and pulling a hoodie up over my head to narrow my visual field and eliminate my peripheral vision. That's not necessary, but it's a hack that has helped me.

Try this right now for yourself. First, look at this book and expand your visual field by trying to see things as far to the left and right as possible without moving your eyes. That will bring your eyes into more of a relaxed state. Then, focus as intently as you can on the words in the book. Think of it like you're trying to look through a toilet paper roll and narrow your gaze so that you don't see anything to the sides. Try blinking as little as possible because that will help make the brain more alert. Focus like this for a few minutes and you will notice your alertness increase.

But you can't do this kind of visual focus forever because eventually your eyes will get tired. It's recommended that after every forty-five minutes of intense visual or mental focus, you relax the eyes by widening your gaze for five minutes. This lets you take in larger areas with less detail. You can also take in the periphery when using a wide visual field, though it's not as clear and you don't see as many details. Look off into the distance or at the horizon to use your panoramic vision. Relaxing your gaze after forty-five minutes of intense focus goes perfectly with the Pomodoro Technique and is part of the reason why the technique is so effective when trying to focus. It's also why it's so important not to look at your phone when you take your five-minute break because that requires narrowing your visual field.

You also want your eyes to be looking up, above nose level, to keep your brain alert.[9] Looking down or below nose level means the neurons in the eyes will activate parts of the brain linked with calm and sleepiness. This makes you less alert, but it's what many people do when they work on their computers—they look down, so their gaze is below nose level. The good news is that we also have neurons that do the opposite, and you activate those by looking above nose level. Doing this will trigger parts of the brain associated with alertness. Therefore, I recommend using an external monitor that is raised a little bit above nose level, to help you remain more alert.

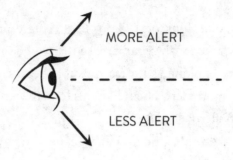

Lighting

Light, especially blue light, does wonders to help us focus, and as mentioned, there is blue light inside normal, white lights as well. We do much of our work during the day, but most of us spend that time cooped up indoors. That's why it's important to make your workspace as bright as possible without your having to squint or be uncomfortable. If you have the option, put your desk near a window. Open that window if you can because an open window will bring in more blue light from the sun to stimulate the eyes. That blue light can have a significant impact on your brain and productivity. Research at Brigham and Women's Hospital found that exposure to blue light directly improves alertness and performance, while also helping to improve memory, cognitive function, and mood.[10] Consistent exposure to blue light during the daytime can help regulate your circadian rhythms and improve your sleep. This is why it's helpful to go outside throughout the day; it's a good way to stimulate the brain for focus.

Sometimes it's not possible to be exposed to blue light when working inside. You don't want the light in your room to be so bright that it's blinding or hurts your eyes, but you want it to be bright. Keep in mind that people have different retinal sensitivities, so some can tolerate more light than others. As a general rule, people with darker eyes tend to tolerate more light than those with lighter eyes.

You also want to have as much overhead light as possible. The reason is because the photoreceptors in the retina called melanopsin ganglion cells, which regulate how our pupils respond to light (among other things), are mainly in the lower half of the retina and view the upper visual field above us. Why? Because the sun is above us, so the idea is to stimulate those cells into thinking the sun is out. When they receive photons from the light, those cells send signals to our brains that create a state of alertness. That's why it is harder to focus and stay alert if you're in a dark room. Just as the light signals the brain to produce hormones corresponding with wakefulness, darkness signals it to produce melatonin.[11] If you don't have access to overhead light, ring lights are inexpensive and have bright blue light that stimulates the various cells in your eyes. I have one that I keep right in front of my screen, above the external monitor on my desk.

When you work inside, try to get outside as much as possible. During breaks, I always go outside to make sure I can take in those photons from the sun. Just being in sunlight tells my eyes and my brain that it's time to be alert and get things done. This doesn't sound like a big deal, but it can make a huge difference to your productivity if you aren't stuck inside all day. A sun lamp can work well too if you can't go outside.

When the sun goes down, you want to dim the lights and adopt a different strategy because exposure to bright light at night can have a negative effect on your circadian rhythms, metabolism, and sleep. So unless you have to work at night, or are just a night owl, this approach to bright light could negatively affect your body clock if you do it at the wrong time of day. Blue light is especially disruptive at night because it's telling the brain to stay alert and delay the release of melatonin, which helps you fall asleep. That is why it's so important to stay off your phone and other devices before bed. A simple rule of thumb: you want to be exposed to light when the sun is up and avoid too much exposure to light after the sun goes down. That will help the brain know when to focus, and when to wind down.

Sound

You can make sound work for your focus in one of two ways—by either enhancing or limiting the sounds around you. Everyone's tolerance for background noise is different, which is why some people like to work at coffee shops and others prefer a quiet library. Your ability to focus with music or background noise also may differ from day to day.

If you need quiet to focus, find spaces that are as private as possible. Noise-canceling headphones can be a great tool. No matter where I go to work, I always take my noise-canceling headphones with me, which signal to people that I don't want to be disturbed.

One practice that I've found helps me concentrate is listening to a specific type of music—or even the same song. When I need to focus, I listen to the same song on repeat. It doesn't have any lyrics, and it's the only song I listen to when I work. In this way, I have trained my brain to know that it's time to focus when I hear it. It's classical conditioning—just like Pavlov's dogs, which were trained to anticipate being fed by the ringing of a bell. You can do this too, so pick out a song that works for you—any song that doesn't have any lyrics. I've found that binaural beats—an audio track with two slightly different frequencies—are another excellent way for me to focus, although the research is mixed on this subject.[12] You can find plenty of examples on Spotify and YouTube.

Certain sounds can enhance focus, and others can distract you, so you have to be careful. Even the hum of an office air conditioner can be a distraction. You might not even realize you can hear it, but it could create a level of stress and anxiety that makes it difficult for you to focus. That's why you may want to avoid white noise in the background if you're looking to focus for extended periods of time. The jury remains out on the effectiveness of white noise.[13]

Bringing music and sound into your work process might require trial and error, and you might find that you focus better without sound because too much sound (or the wrong type of sound) can be distracting, and that's counterproductive. But give it a try to see what works for you.

Accountability Partner

Finding someone who can help keep you accountable as you take action is a fantastic way to make progress toward achieving your goals.

It's awesome when you have the same goals as a close friend. If those goals are related to fitness and health, you can go to the gym together and put together the same diet and nutrition plan, while giving each other added motivation and making sure the other person sticks to that plan. I have a best friend and business partner whom I've worked with for the past fifteen years who serves this function in my life. We've grown together, and we've held each other accountable to our goals. I wouldn't have achieved those goals without him.

It's great if you have a person like that in your life, but it's not always possible. I get messages from people all the time telling me that nobody in their family has the same goals, and they feel like an odd duck among their friends. This is why it helps to surround yourself with people who have similar goals, but if you don't have those people in your life yet, it's no big deal. All you need is someone who will hold you accountable. Think of your most annoying friend who will call you out when you're wrong and hold your feet to the fire. That can be the perfect person. Let's say that you want to lose weight by working out four times a week. It doesn't matter if this friend is severely out of shape. Simply tell that person you will send them a selfie from the gym four times a week or you will pay them $100 every time you don't. That's a great accountability partner because you know that person will make sure you're doing what you're supposed to since they get paid if you don't. It also makes you more likely to hold up your end of the bargain and do what you said you would because you'll be out money if you don't. Who is that friend for you, and what arrangement can you reach that will guarantee that person will hold you accountable?

Another way an accountability partner can help is when you simply report back to them your progress. Pearson's Law says that when performance is measured, performance improves; but when performance is measured and reported, that rate of improvement accelerates. In other words, don't only track your progress, but enlist someone who holds you accountable, and you will get exponentially better.

One of my clients had a goal to lose thirty pounds, and I used Pearson's Law to help him. I'm not a fitness coach or trainer, so I wasn't going to give him any diet or exercise tips, but I suggested that he buy a scale that was connected to his phone through Bluetooth. Every morning, he would get on that scale, which would show him his weight and a whole host of beneficial facts, but the crucial first step was to measure his progress. Before we spoke at the end of the week, he would send me a screenshot of every weigh-in. That held him accountable and gave him an extra incentive, so on the days when he wasn't making progress or slid back a little, he knew that he had to push himself harder. It worked, and in the first four months, he exceeded his goals and went from 230 pounds down to 195.

You can't expect to be motivated every day. There will be days when you aren't feeling it and don't want to do what you need to do. Accountability partners will give you the added push to dig down and get it done. And nowhere does it say you must have only one accountability partner. When it comes to getting others to help you achieve your goals, you want as many people in your corner to support you as possible.

Movement

Inaction leads to more inaction, and action leads to more action (and motivation follows action), so consider these last two tools—movement and cold water—the ones you use during your SOS moments.

Sometimes when you aren't feeling it, you just have to *move*. Get up, move your body, and do something to increase your heart rate. That might be walking around the block, doing one hundred jumping jacks, or finding a ten-minute workout on YouTube. Turn on some music and dance around the room if you want to get your body moving and your heart rate up.

According to psychiatry professor John Ratney at Harvard Medical School, "We know exercise improves our ability to think,"[14] which includes working memory, prioritizing, and sustaining attention. He found that exercise can improve your focus for two to three hours. Not only does exercise improve mood, sleep, and overall health, but it increases blood flow, which translates to more oxygen, and ultimately more energy. The hippocampus is activated during exercise, which is critical for learning and memory. A 2015 study in Dutch schoolchildren between the ages of ten and thirteen found that those who completed two twenty-minute sessions of moderate exercise performed better on selective attention tests.[15]

Moving your body creates that essential momentum and motivation to do the activity you need to get done. Break the cycle of inaction by taking action (like typing something—it doesn't even matter what that action is), and it will be easier to keep taking action.

Movement helps in so many ways. Try changing up where you do your work. Some people have discovered they focus better when they change their workplace location after each task. Simply moving to a different seat or a different room reinvigorates them and creates a sense of heightened alertness.

Cold Water

People hate this one, but I can promise you that it's much more effective than chugging a cup of coffee. Jumping into cold water or doing an ice plunge (as long as you can do it in a safe environment) or taking a cold shower can boost your levels of dopamine—the molecule that helps you feel motivated. Research showed that one hour of head-out immersion in water at fourteen degrees Celsius (fifty-seven degrees Fahrenheit) increased dopamine concentration by 250 percent![16] When dopamine levels are high, you want to put in the work to get things done. We'll talk about dopamine in Part III.

Cold water is also a great way to get you energized to do those things you don't want to do. When I'm feeling unmotivated or experiencing an SOS moment, I do one hundred jumping jacks and then jump into my forty-degree cold plunge pool for four minutes. After that, I feel like I can run through a wall, no matter how tired or unmotivated I felt before.

* * *

These seven tools can help you to develop your own routine to focus and get things done. They can be especially helpful on days when you struggle to find your motivation, so try them all out to see which ones work best for you. You want a few of these in your tool belt because they will come in handy when we put it all together in the next chapter.

Journal Prompts

- Write down the needle-moving actions you need to complete regularly to significantly increase your productivity.

- As you test out each of the seven tools discussed in this chapter, describe your experiences in your journal and write about whether each helped you focus and how.

- Make a list of who might make good accountability buddies for you and how. Brainstorm the kind of arrangements you could make with each person so that they would hold you accountable to your goals.

- What will you do to incorporate these seven tools into your daily routine? Write down the commitments you can make to yourself, or with your accountability buddy.

For more journal prompts and video lessons from this book, go to: https://RobDial.com/LevelUp.

Part III

CREATING HABITS AND MAKING THEM STICK

Understanding why you don't take action and developing a plan to use micro-actions will get you far, but you won't achieve success until you learn how to sustain your momentum.

Have you ever been really excited to start something only to give up on your goal a few days or weeks later? Too many people start off strong but never finish what they set out to accomplish because they can't sustain the changes they try to make in their lives. It's time to stop that. This is the last obstacle standing in the way between you and success.

The trick is making your brain work for you instead of against you. Fortunately, your brain changes and adapts through its ability to form and reorganize synaptic connections—called *neuroplasticity*.

Combining the brain's neuroplasticity with the knowledge of how to create a dopamine reward system will help you fall in love with taking action. When that happens, you will no longer have to force yourself to take action because it will come naturally. That's how you will level up.

CHAPTER 9

Consistency

How to Show Up Every Day

When I was nineteen years old and working in sales, there was a period when I started to slack off. I wasn't making the calls or doing the work I needed to. Worse, I was making excuses and laying blame elsewhere for not being where I wanted to be in life. When I vented to my coach at the time, he asked me, "If you look at a business, and it's not succeeding, whose fault is that?"

"The CEO's," I told him.

"What if that business is succeeding, and all the thousands of people in that company help move the needle forward—who's responsible for that?"

"The CEO," I said again.

"So, if you get to the end of your life and realize that things didn't turn out the way you wanted—you didn't get the happiness, love, or have all the experiences you wished you could have had—whose fault is that?"

"I guess it's my fault."

"And if you become a huge success, have a positive impact on the world, and achieve everything you set out to achieve, who would be responsible for that?"

"Me."

"The reason why you aren't getting what you want right now is that you aren't treating your life like a business. You have to learn how to become the CEO of your own life because if things aren't going the way you want, it's nobody's fault but your own."

This piece of advice changed the trajectory of my life more than any other piece of advice I have ever been given. At that moment, my life started to change. I stopped making excuses and approached things from a different perspective. The more I did that, the more I realized that the actions I was taking (or not taking) every day did not line up with where I wanted to go and the person I wanted to be. I realized that if I wanted to change my life, it started with the little choices I made and actions I took or didn't take every day. You can either make excuses or get results. There is no other option, and you can't do both, so you must make a choice.

> You can either make excuses or get results.

Sixteen years later, I can now look back and see that I made the right choice. I've gotten to where I am today not because of any big event, but because of those micro-actions that I consistently took to create routines in my life. Although many of those actions may have seemed insignificant at the time, those were the actions that mattered the most and had the most impact because they compounded over time.

French chef Fernand Point said, "Success is the sum of all the things done correctly." Another quote, attributed to Theodore Roosevelt, expresses a similar philosophy: "It is the little things well done that go to make up a truly successful and good life."

Success means different things to different people. To some, it means making a million dollars. To others, it means having a family or being able to support themselves as an artist. It doesn't matter what you're trying to do, you don't have to be the smartest, fastest, or most talented person to reach your goals. You just have to be the most consistent. If you show up for yourself every day, if you're aimed in the right direction and taking the right action, you will eventually hit your goals. Yet for many people, this is the part where they get stuck.

> It doesn't matter what you're trying to do,
> you don't have to be the smartest, fastest,
> or most talented person to reach your goals.
> You just have to be the most consistent.

I get messages all the time from people saying they set a goal and do well for a week or two before they fall off. Does this resonate with you? Many of these same people tell me that they struggle with consistency, but that's actually inaccurate. "I struggle with consistency" is an identity statement. Start paying attention to the words you say, especially when it comes to identity statements like these because as we explored in Part I, your actions will always line up with your identity. You might have struggled with consistency in the past, but it's not part of your identity now. So, if you're someone who says "I struggle with consistency," tell yourself instead, "I struggled with consistency in the past, but I am working to become more consistent every single day." I've struggled to be consistent in the past as well, but that doesn't mean I have to struggle with it in the present or future.

Most people struggle to be consistent because they don't have the tools to help them. That's what this chapter is all about, and it starts by changing the way you think about discipline.

The Secret to Discipline

You might not be in sales, but when you're trying to talk yourself out of doing something, I'll bet you become the best salesperson in the world. Whenever we're faced with something hard, that voice in our head immediately wants to negotiate. Here's a tip: Never negotiate with your own mind! One of the main reasons why people have so much trouble taking action is because they negotiate with their minds and have been letting their mind win for most of their lives.

The one thing that drowns out that voice in your head is discipline, but what exactly is discipline? For some, discipline has a bad connotation—like having to discipline a child or a dog when they misbehave—but I don't think of it as a bad thing at all. I think of discipline as self-love because it takes discipline to do things that I know are good for me. Discipline has two components: (1) doing what you say you will do, and (2) doing what you need to do, even when you don't want to do it.

One common excuse I often hear people say is "If I had a job that I loved, I would be more disciplined," or "When I have my own business, then I will be disciplined." Think about this for a second because it doesn't make any sense. Discipline doesn't come from doing the things you *want* to do—it comes from doing the things you don't want to do but know that you *should* do. If you're truly trying to build discipline, you should build it while working at that job you hate. If you can perform at a high level there, you'll kill it once you start doing what you love.

We might not realize it, but we've been training ourselves to be undisciplined and give up our entire lives. Have you ever taken out the trash and dropped something along the way? You immediately tell yourself that someone else will get it. Have you tried on a bunch of outfits and then left them on the bed, assuming that you will put them away later? How about lounging on the couch and talking yourself out of something that you know you need to do? Of course. We all do it. You're not alone. That voice in your head will always try to resist, but the trick is not to listen to it or try to negotiate with yourself. The trick is to lean into that resistance. Why? Because action breeds action, and inaction breeds inaction.

Just like we've trained ourselves to give up, we can also train ourselves to become disciplined. The hard part is breaking the cycle of inaction to get started. It seems daunting, but the solution is simple: *just get moving*. I'm not saying you have to go do all the things you need to get done. Just do *something*. Get your body physically moving. Do push-ups or jumping jacks. Take a walk around the block. When you move, the chemicals in your body change. Your heartbeat and your breath change, and that prepares you both physically and mentally to move in the direction you want to go.

Mel Robbins wrote *The 5 Second Rule* about this very concept: if you have to do something, count down from five and then physically move. I had been doing something similar for years, but I was counting down from three. I was shy as a kid. I knew that if I ever wanted to make friends and have girlfriends, I'd have to learn how to talk to people, but I'd get nervous and not say anything when I had the chance. So, what I did was focus on the first word I had to say to initiate conversation, count down from three, *and just say it.*

I still do this in many different circumstances today, but it's not nearly as difficult because I've trained myself not to negotiate with my mind. I don't allow myself to stop and think. I just go. It happens almost daily when it's time to work out because I hate working out. I've never been a guy who can't wait to go to the gym. The words "Oh yay, it's leg day" have never come out of my mouth. There are so many other things that I would rather do, and I have plenty of excuses, but I force myself to work out. That starts by moving. Just moving. When I get to the gym, I still encounter resistance. That voice in my head is telling me all of the reasons why I need to cut out early, but I do just a little more. One more set. One more exercise. That's when the chemicals in my brain and body begin to change, and it gets easier. I even want to stay longer. By the end, I feel great, and I'm glad that I got up and went to the gym!

Another trick to help you take action is to just get your foot in the door. For example, I hate doing the dishes. I hate it even more than going to the gym. I hate it more than laundry, which is saying a lot. However, it always (almost) gets done because of this trick: instead of thinking of all the dishes I need to wash, I simply tell myself that I'm going to wash one dish. That's it. I literally wash only one dish. Why? Because once I wash one dish and put it away, I'm like, *Okay, I'll do another one.* So, I do. And then I wash another and another. Pretty soon, I'm focused on finishing all of the dishes. It might not work every time, but all you have to do is succeed more than you don't to create that positive momentum.

That initial mental resistance holds so many people back and prevents them from taking action, but if you can get your foot in the door by just starting to do the act, you begin to chip away at that mental resistance.

The people who are the most successful are the ones who consistently try to do just a little bit more and be a little bit better. They push themselves past what is possible because there is always another level. If you look at life like that, it doesn't matter what you're trying to do; you will transform into a brand-new version of yourself who might be unrecognizable to you now. The hardest part is getting started.

Another trick is to get in the habit of finishing what you start, even the little things. I make the bed in the morning to finish the act of sleeping. I wash the dishes after a meal to finish the act of eating. I put away my clean clothes to finish the act of doing laundry. None of these things will change my life, but I'm training my brain to finish what I start. If you approach everything in your life like this, in six months you will have created discipline, and that will better prepare you to finish the bigger things. But the real secret is not to stop when you said you would—go above and beyond, and make that a habit so you can build momentum.

Once when I was on the treadmill at the gym, I had planned to run for ten minutes and found myself about to hit the button and turn off the treadmill at 9:50 when something clicked in my head, and I knew that I had to keep going all the way to ten minutes. It seems so small. We're talking about only ten seconds. Nobody else would have known or cared whether I hit that button and stopped. Physically, it wouldn't have made much difference, but mentally I was setting myself up for failure. I realized that if I was stopping short of my goals at the gym, I was probably also stopping short of my goals in life. I believe that the way you do one thing in life is the way you do everything. From that day forward, I set out to do more than I said I would—1 percent more.

At the gym, doing 1 percent more means running for a few more seconds on the treadmill or pushing for one or two more reps. Not everything is quantifiable, so often, doing 1 percent more simply means that when I go to bed at night, I make sure that I've leveled up and am in a better place than the day before. This change is often un-recognizable at the moment but pays dividends when compounded over time. Most important, it conditions your brain to not only finish things, but to go beyond what you need to do.

Discipline is one of the most important skills required to achieve success because the more disciplined you are, the more you can take action, which means the more you get done, and the more quickly you change your life.

Discipline isn't found in the job you love; it's created through the tiny things that you do every day, regardless of how you feel. I firmly believe that the way you do one thing is the way you do everything. It doesn't matter how big or small, because if you aren't going to do those little things, how do you expect to do the big things when you encounter resistance? It all starts by not thinking of discipline in a negative way and realizing that it's a form of self-love. But discipline isn't the only tool in your tool kit.

Set Yourself Free Through Ritual

One simple way to become more consistent is by developing rituals. A ritual is a meaningful practice or routine that has a framework and a step-by-step process. It's intentional, planned, and, when used strategically and repeatedly, will get you closer to your goals. Some people resist rituals because they believe that they are restrictive and dull. People like novelty and want to switch up their routine, which is great to do at times, but most successful people know that rituals create freedom. It sounds counterintuitive at first, but just like we've been discussing throughout this book, the road to success is all about putting in some work on the front end that will make the journey easier down the road. Rituals done now create more freedom in the future.

Think of it this way: If you develop a workout or movement ritual that you practice every day, you will become healthier and that will lead to a future with more movement. If you develop a consistent study ritual now, you will get better grades, creating more opportunities for yourself in the future. If you develop a consistent work ritual now, you will make more money and enjoy more important responsibilities down the road.

You can swap in just about any example and see that developing consistent rituals in the present will lead to more free time later. And there is nothing people want more than freedom. Some people may think what they most want is money, but those people often really want the freedom that comes with that money. We all want the freedom to do what we want, with whom we want, when we want. We want the freedom to not worry about paying rent next month. We want the freedom to go on a trip with our friends next weekend without checking our bank account to see whether it's feasible. We want the freedom to buy a present for our partner without having to pinch pennies for the next couple of months. That's the freedom most people seek, and that's the freedom you can achieve when you develop good rituals now.

> We all want the freedom to do what we
> want, with whom we want, when we want.

Professional athletes are known for their rituals. Some are small: LeBron James throws chalk up into the air before games. Tiger Woods wore a red shirt on Sundays for the final round of a tournament. Michael Jordan wore shorts from his national championship season at the University of North Carolina under his Bulls uniform throughout his NBA career. Some athletes' rituals are more about consistent practice, such as Wade Boggs's ritual: The third baseman took the field at the same time every night. He fielded exactly 150 ground balls before beginning batting practice at 5:17 p.m. and then ran wind sprints at 7:17 p.m. He visualized four different at bats and saw himself getting four consecutive hits. He believed that mentally prepared him to play every night, and with good reason because the science backs it up. A 2017 study showed that rituals improve performance.[1] And now Boggs is in the Hall of Fame.

Focus on creating a ritual for those daily needle-moving activities that you write on your index card. Let's create a sample ritual to see how you might do this. Suppose that you need to sit down and do two hours of focused work to complete a presentation. You can turn getting ready for your work into a ritual by doing the following actions in this order:

1. Clear your workspace of clutter.

2. Eliminate distractions in your physical space and put your phone away.

3. Set up the proper lighting.

4. Keep your notebook nearby to jot down any unrelated thoughts that come to mind.

5. Put on your noise-canceling headphones.

6. Take six deep breaths.

7. Narrow your vision field by staring at your computer screen for two minutes.

You are now ready to start your work, whether by using the Pomodoro Technique or other focusing strategies.

Even if you're working on a variety of projects, you want to maintain the same ritual every single time you begin your work. Take this ritual seriously. If you treat it like something sacred, it will become important. This will condition your brain over time. Even if it feels difficult at first, if you stick with it, soon the ritual will become more natural, and you'll encounter less resistance when trying to focus and begin work.

Try out the example above or come up with a ritual of your own. The same process can apply to any number of activities; if you want to learn to play a song on the piano, for example, you can follow the same process (except maybe not the noise-canceling headphones).

Micro-Actions Create Macro Results

As we discussed earlier, success is not one big event that changes your life. It's the accumulation of all the micro-actions you take every day.

It all goes back to those three main components: direction, action, and time (see Chapter 5). When you make good decisions and take the right actions, time is your best friend. When you make bad decisions that take you further away from your goals, time is your worst enemy. That's what makes time the great equalizer. It will show you the result of the actions you have taken in the past. Everything works itself out in time, so if you take the right actions now, you will love your future, but if you don't, you won't. It's that simple.

What makes this so difficult to wrap our heads around is that those little daily micro-actions don't necessarily produce immediate results. However, when compounded over ten years, for instance, they will completely change the trajectory of your life. In his book *The Compound Effect*, Darren Hardy writes, "It's not the big things that add up in the end; it's the hundreds, thousands, or millions of little things that separate the ordinary from the extraordinary."[2] Huge rewards and radical change come from small, smart choices made consistently over time. The problem is that most people don't think like this.

> Huge rewards and radical change come from small, smart choices made consistently over time.

When asked whether they would rather have a million dollars or a penny doubled every day for a month, most people pick the million dollars without realizing that a penny doubled every day for thirty days comes out to $5,368,709.12. Here's another way to think about the power of compounding: If you deposit $1,000 and earn 10 percent interest over a year, your account balance will increase to $1,100. The following year, you'll be earning interest on your original deposit and the interest. In the short term, it might not seem like much, but after twenty-five years, that account increases to $10,835. After fifty years, you will have $117,391 in the bank. Micro-actions work the same way.

Here are the top examples I've come across in my own life and during work as a coach:

- Deciding to go to bed early today so you can wake up early tomorrow is a micro-action that will have little immediate effect at the moment, but over years it will free up more time for you to do what you want and help you create healthy habits.

- If you read ten pages today, it won't make you more intelligent, but if you make that a habit every day for ten years, it will have a significant effect. If the average book is three hundred pages long, that adds up to reading 120 books over the next ten years.

- Meeting with your sales team for fifteen minutes today isn't going to move the needle much, but hold that same fifteen-minute meeting every day, and you will create a cohesive sales team that is on top of their game.

- Studying Spanish for thirty minutes today will not make you a fluent Spanish speaker. But study for thirty minutes every day for ten years—that's 1,825 hours of studying Spanish, which will go a ways toward being fluent.

- Meditating for ten minutes today won't immediately lessen your anxious mind, but meditating for ten minutes a day every day for the next ten years means that you will have meditated for 608 hours. The long-term result of that can mean you become a less anxious and more peaceful version of yourself.

- Saving $5 today isn't going to make you rich, but saving $5 a day for the next ten years will add $18,250 in your bank account. Take that same money and invest it, and it can increase exponentially over time.

- Eating just one fatty bacon cheeseburger today will not hurt your health, but if you choose the unhealthy option over the healthy choice every day, you'll find that poor nutrition compounded over time can lead to serious health issues. Conversely, eating one healthy meal a day for ten years adds up, too.

- Smoking cigarettes is another example—both the potential health problems and the expense, when compounded over time, take your life down different paths, one of which you probably don't want to find yourself on in the future. Different actions will lead you to a different destination.

If you make micro-actions part of your consistent rituals, even for just minutes a day, your life will change over time. You will find yourself in a completely different place. Whether that place is positive or negative depends on the action you take.

Your life comes down to three to five important actions each day. It's easy to get overwhelmed when we think about all the things we have to do and don't know where to start. If you limit yourself to three decisions (at most, five) that turn into three actions, you're on your way. For example, waking up when the alarm goes off instead of hitting snooze, working out instead of creating an excuse, and making one hundred prospecting calls instead of worrying about the possibility of being rejected are all decisions that help bring you closer to your goals. Sometimes it's as simple as putting away your phone so you can be present with your kids, or choosing to give your significant other a compliment, that can make the most difference. Focus on those most important decisions because when repeated daily, those are the difference between a good life and a great life. It's easy to believe that the poor decisions we make in the moment aren't big deals. It's just a hamburger. It's just skipping a workout. It's just not meditating, reading, or saving money today. We can blind ourselves to ways those small decisions have an impact on our future when compounded. Napoleon Hill said, "If you cannot do great things, do small things in a great way."

> "If you cannot do great things, do small things in a great way." —Napoleon Hill

Technology has made much of what we do more convenient, and so many things are now available with the click of a button that we've almost come to expect that's how life can always be. But fitness, success, joy, peace, happiness, and health don't work like that. There is no immediate payoff. They take time. It goes back to the question: Do you want things to be easy now and hard later, or hard now and easy later? So, if you want a different future, you must adopt different micro-actions today. That's why I don't care about where you are now. I care about *what you're doing* right now because that will determine where you will be. The one thing you don't want to do is wait to get started.

It all goes back to that quotation from James Clear (see Part II): "Every action you take is a vote for the person you wish to become." If you choose the bacon cheeseburger over the salad, that's a vote for the person you want to become. And I love how Clear uses the word "vote" because you don't have to get 100 percent of the votes to win an election. You don't need to be perfect. You need to get only the majority—51 percent at the least. Obviously, the more actions you take in the right direction, the better; but I'm not saying that you must pick the salad over the hamburger every time. All you have to do is make sure you're headed in the right direction most of the time. Step by step and day by day you will eventually get there. This is a long game, and slow and steady wins the race.

Strive for Consistent Progress, Not Perfection

Suppose you walk into a friend's garage and see that he has dozens of beautiful paintings that he created. You're in shock and tell him, "I had no idea you could paint this well! You should try to sell them or put them on Instagram. People need to see these."

"No, no, no," he says. "They aren't ready yet. They need more work."

"What are you talking about? These are great! What more work could you possibly do?"

"I can't help it. I'm a perfectionist."

Ah, there it is! The problem isn't that the paintings need work. The problem is that your friend identifies himself as a perfectionist. That's his identity statement. Here's a secret: perfection doesn't exist. Out of the tens of thousands of people I've worked with and coached, almost all of them consider themselves perfectionists. So, if you think you're a perfectionist, welcome to the club, but don't ever strive to achieve perfection because you will never be perfect.

The real reason your friend doesn't want to show his artwork to the world is that he's afraid of what people might think. What if someone thinks his paintings are ugly? What if he's judged? What if he's rejected? What if he does put them in a gallery or open a pop-up show and nobody buys anything? What if he prices them at $1,000 each and he overhears someone laugh and say to their friend, "I wouldn't pay $10 for that piece of crap"? These thoughts hold him back and prevent him from putting himself out there. It's easy for him to say "They're not ready yet" because that doesn't force him to face that fear. That's why perfectionism is the enemy of creativity and also the enemy of taking action. It's good to have high standards, but it's not doing you any good when you allow perfectionism to prevent you from bringing your light into the world.

I work with many people who think this way about trying to create motivational and educational videos to post on social media. They have every excuse in the world to not get them done—the lighting isn't right, the script needs work—but they're actually worried about being judged. That's at the root of perfectionism, so if you tell yourself that you can't get started or aren't yet ready to work toward your goals because the circumstances aren't perfect, you're lying to yourself and trying to cover up some kind of fear or insecurity. Perfectionism is a mask you wear to hide a fear.

> Perfectionism is a mask you wear to hide a fear.

I've learned this the hard way, battling perfectionism for most of my life. I demand the best, and anything short of "this is amazing!" isn't acceptable. But it's impossible to live life like that. When I first created my podcast, I recorded some episodes and then tinkered and played around with ideas but never released anything. Finally, eight months later, I said, "You know what, I don't care what anybody else says. I want to do this, and people can judge me if they want."

And that's precisely what they did. If you listen to my first few episodes, they were awful. I still remember my first negative review. It said something like "For someone who is a motivational speaker, this guy has got the most unmotivating voice I've ever heard." My first thought was *To hell with her!* I was pissed, but then I looked at the episodes more closely and wondered whether she was right. I wasn't on point. I spoke in a monotone, and I didn't sound like myself. Because of that review, I adjusted and got better. That still happens. I'm more than thirteen hundred episodes in, and I'm still learning, growing, and adapting. None of this would have happened had I waited for everything to be perfect and not put myself out there.

One of my mentors used to tell me that "done is better than perfect." Getting something done will help you get where you want to go more quickly than toiling over it and waiting for it to be perfect.

And guess what? Nobody wants perfectionism. If you listen to my podcast, it's riddled with mistakes. I mess up, fumble with my words, and repeat myself, but that's what people like. They tell me it feels like they're having a conversation with me in their living room. It's not highly edited or produced. That authenticity helps me stand out, and that's gotten me over my fears that were masked in my perfectionism.

Much of life is about taking two, three, four steps forward and then one or two steps back. That doesn't mean that it's okay to give up, but mistakes are going to happen. We're human, so it's inevitable. What matters is how you respond to messing up. If your goal is to go on a diet to lose weight, and you crush it for six-and-a-half days but then slip up, you can respond in one of two ways. You can judge yourself, which can create a downward spiral that demotivates you. Or you can have a meeting with yourself: Admit to messing up, but show yourself some grace, and adjust accordingly, so you can avoid making the same mistake again. Shift your focus onto the six-and-a-half days of incredible progress and not the tiny one-day mess-up. Build yourself up so you can get back on track and headed in the right direction as quickly as possible.

> Consistency is better than perfection.

Ditch the mask covering up your insecurity because perfectionism is not self-improvement—it's trying to gain approval by looking perfect. It will hinder your success and limit your progress, and remember, it's impossible to achieve. There will always be haters, and you will always be judged, so you might as well take your best shot instead of holding yourself back. You are never going to be perfect, and that is perfectly normal. Embrace it, and focus on making consistent progress, not trying to achieve perfection. I will take that one step further and say that consistency is better than perfection. At a college commencement address, Jim Carrey said, "Your need for acceptance can make you invisible in this world." You weren't born to be invisible. You were born to bring your unique gifts into the world.

* * *

Success is like growing Chinese bamboo: First you plant it in fertilized soil, give it plenty of sunshine, and water it every day for a year, and then . . . nothing! It doesn't even sprout up above the soil, and you keep doing the same thing repeatedly without seeing any results until, finally, during the fifth year, it explodes! It grows up to eighty feet in only six weeks and can grow two feet in a single day. That's so fast you can almost see it grow. Success in life works the same way. From the outside, we might see someone we think is an overnight success, but in reality, successful people work hard for years without anyone seeing it. They do it in the dark, so people see only the eighty feet of growth in six weeks, but the eighty feet of growth is not the most impressive feat. The five years of work that made that massive growth happen is most important.

It starts by bringing more self-awareness to your decisions and the actions you take (or don't take). Don't wait for things to be perfect before getting started, and don't excuse poor choices in the moment that aren't getting you where you want to go. As long as you're pointed in the right direction, any action is better than no action. Remember, every action is a vote for the person you want to become. This isn't a sprint; slow and steady wins the race, so don't try to fly out of the gates. All you have to do is make sure you're going in the right direction and taking the right actions because time will be on your side. When you lie down every night to sleep, get in the habit of asking yourself, *Did I get 1 percent better today?* That's what matters most because if you want your life to change, you must be the one to change it.

> If you want your life to change,
> you must be the one to change it.

Journal Prompts

Take a day or two to observe your behavior while paying close attention to the little things you do—sometimes without even thinking. Remember how you tracked your energy every hour by setting a timer? Try something similar here. This way you can stop to log your actions in smaller increments throughout the day. This can help you become better acquainted with your own tendencies because sometimes, we aren't aware of how we might be sabotaging our own progress. With a clear grasp of your behavior, take time to journal about these questions:

- What micro-actions do you need to take daily to bring you closer to your goals?

- What micro-actions do you take daily that take you further away from your goals?

- What ways might you excuse or justify those negative micro-actions?

- How can you replace those negative micro-actions with positive micro-actions in the future?

For more journal prompts and video lessons from this book, go to:
https://RobDial.com/LevelUp.

CHAPTER 10

Habits

How to Make Taking Action Effortless

When the show *Seinfeld* first aired, Jerry Seinfeld continued to work as a touring stand-up comic. Before he went onstage one night, he was approached by a young comedian looking to break through. That comedian saw an opportunity, so he asked Seinfeld whether he had any advice for someone just starting out.

Seinfeld told him that he needed good jokes, which sounds obvious, but he emphasized that you get better jokes by writing every day. Seinfeld knew that if he wrote every day, even just a little bit, he would eventually develop a massive portfolio of material. There would be some duds, but he would still come up with some great jokes. He learned that working every day, as if he had a regular day job, was more effective than writing only during an extended cram session or waiting for inspiration. Compounded over months and years, that daily writing couldn't help but improve his craft. But he also had a trick. It's a method that became known as the Seinfeld Strategy.

JANUARY

SUN	MON	TUE	WED	THU	FRI	SAT
X 1	X 2	X 3	X 4	X 5	X 6	X 7
X 8	X 9	10	11	12	13	14
15	16	17	18	19	20	21
22	23	24	25	26	27	28
29	30	31				

Seinfeld bought a very large calendar with the entire year on one page. He put it where he knew that he would see it multiple times a day. Every day that he sat down to write, he would take a red Magic Marker and put an X through that day. Eventually, he would have a chain of red Xs, and that would motivate him to keep the chain going. The motivation became stronger the longer the chain got because he had visual proof of his progress. What was beautiful about this system was that after a while, Seinfeld didn't have to force himself to sit down and write. There was no resistance. It became natural, so he didn't have to think about it. It doesn't matter whether you're writing jokes, working out, growing your business, or trying to eat healthier foods; when you repeat rituals and micro-actions, they become habits.

What is a habit? It's something that your brain and body do

unconsciously. It's something you've done so many times that it's become reflexive. It's a voluntary action that is controlled by your subconscious mind. Two Harvard psychologists determined that 47 percent of what we do every day is habitual and done on autopilot.[1] Some studies have found an even higher percentage.

Have you ever left work or driven home from somewhere and arrived with almost no memory of the trip? You were awake but on autopilot. Have you ever shut the door or turned the lights off after leaving a room without even thinking about it? I do this all the time and sometimes turn the lights off when my wife is still in a room. The reason is that when I was a kid, my mom would get so angry about wasting money on electricity that she trained me to always turn the lights off when I left a room. Now that action is automatic.

This is what you want to happen with your positive needle-moving micro-actions. By practicing deliberate rituals, you can turn them into habits, so they require less intention, conscious thought, and effort. Imagine how much you could accomplish if all of those little things that you need to do every day to get you moving in the right direction occurred without your even thinking about them. That can happen, but it helps to understand what's going on in the brain so you can use that to your advantage.

Your brain makes up only about 2 percent of your body weight, but it expends about 20 percent of your daily energy supply, making it the most energy-consuming organ in your body.[2] That's why you're fried after a long day of making phone calls, attending meetings, writing, answering emails, and doing all the things that require brainpower, even if you never get up from your seat.

The brain doesn't want to do any more work than necessary, and the way it conserves energy is by recognizing patterns and creating shortcuts. And the more you do something, the more ingrained that pattern becomes in your brain, which is why breaking from a pattern is so hard. You're asking your brain to do something new, step by step, which the brain resists, wanting you to get back to the usual pattern. If you've ever intended to stop for milk on your drive home from work but forgot about it until you reached your driveway, this is why. Fortunately, you can also use the brain's desire to create patterns and shortcuts to your advantage.

The late Australian actor F. Matthias Alexander is credited with saying, "People do not decide their futures; they decide their habits and their habits decide their future." If you can take advantage of how the brain creates habits in your everyday life, you will have a new superpower.

However, the brain does this unconsciously, so not all habits and patterns are as harmless as driving home from work, and not all habits are positive. Of all the things you do on autopilot every day, how many make it harder for you to achieve your goals in the long run? How many habits do you have that bring you down and hold you back without your even realizing it? As you begin to unravel the wires in your brain to see what you really think and where those thoughts come from, you'll notice many negative patterns that you need to change. But don't worry, you aren't doomed—because you can control your brain. And the first step is taking stock of your habits—both good and bad.

Identifying Your Habits

Brushing your teeth every morning and night is a good habit. Reaching for an alcoholic drink or a cigarette when you feel stressed out is a bad habit. Reaching for a drink or a cigarette at particular times because "that's when I have a drink or cigarette" is a really bad habit. We all have plenty of good and bad habits, so before focusing on all the habits you want to create, you first need to audit your existing habits, so you can get rid of the ones that are not serving you.

How do you do this? It's simple. Ask yourself, "Is this behavior bringing me closer to or sending me further away from my goals?" If your goal is to build up your business, and you find yourself checking Instagram every time you have a few extra minutes, that's a bad habit you want to break. It's not harming you, but it's not bringing you any closer to achieving your goals, and that can have a negative impact on your future by wasting your time, attention, and brainpower. So you want to replace that habit with something that will help you achieve the success you want. For instance, you could have a business book close at hand that you crack open instead of checking social media. Spending those few minutes learning how to grow your business is getting you closer to your goals. Get in the habit of having a business book with you every time you leave the house.

If your goal is to lose ten pounds but you find yourself munching on potato chips and junk food at night, break that bad habit by replacing all the junk food in your house with healthy snacks. For instance, put fruit on a counter that is visible and within reach, so you always have a healthy alternative. Also, most people don't realize that 75 percent of eating is driven by emotions, not hunger.[3] If you're eating because you're bored or stressed out, try to break that habit by first becoming mindful of when and why you reach toward food, then give yourself plenty of options that will get you moving toward your goals instead of away from them.

If your goal is to become a better parent, and one of your bad habits is letting your emotions get the best of you and yelling every time your kids act up, get in the habit of taking yourself out of that moment. Try resetting yourself with six deep breaths, so you can then react from a place of love instead of from an emotionally triggered state. This is difficult for some parents because they learned the habit of yelling at their kids from their own parents. They may not even see it as a habit, just the natural way of parenting. You can be the one to break this habit in your family.

If your goal is to start running early every morning, but one of your habits is staying up late watching TV, replace that habit by giving yourself a cutoff time at the end of the day so you can arrange your clothes, prep for the following day, and get to sleep earlier. You will wake up feeling more refreshed and be able to get out of bed and go for a run!

Everything I teach comes down to intention, but the first step to becoming more intentional is better understanding your own tendencies because you might not even realize what bad habits are holding you back. We started this process already in Chapter 8 by taking a closer look at our daily micro-actions. Once you become aware of your habits and know what you want to change, it becomes easier to catch yourself and change course. The more you do this, the more natural it becomes.

Keystone Habits

One mistake I see people make when they learn about habits is they try to completely overhaul their lives with a bunch of new habits that they assume will help them achieve their goals faster. They try to change so much that they succeed only in sabotaging themselves because the change is too drastic. Their old self resists, and they can't get any of the new habits to stick. You want to focus on the habits that will be the most life-changing and then make them as easy as possible to perform. Don't try to implement a bunch all at once; focus on only one. This is what's called a keystone habit, a term that was first coined by Charles Duhigg in his book *The Power of Habit: Why We Do What We Do in Life and Business.*

An arch made of bricks or stones stays together because of that one stone in the middle, the keystone. Without it, the arch would collapse. Habits work the same way. Once you identify and incorporate into your life a strong keystone habit, it can affect many other areas of your life.

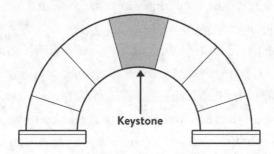

Here's how it works. Let's say that you start waking up early to perform a morning routine. The keystone habit is waking up early, but you don't want to wake up two hours earlier than usual and load up your morning with some intricate routine that involves working out, reading, journaling, and meditating if you aren't used to doing any of those things in the morning, never mind getting up two hours earlier than usual. Your existing identity will fight back, and if you can't check every box, you'll start to feel bad about yourself, and it will only be a matter of time before all those hoped-for habits fall by the wayside.

Instead, keep it simple. Focus only on the keystone habit and wake up early until that becomes normal. Try to do it for one hundred days in a row. I suggest this many days because studies show that it takes on average sixty-six to one hundred days to create a habit—sometimes longer and sometimes shorter, depending on the person and the habit.[4] Shooting for one hundred days will help ensure that habit gets locked in. And that means every day, not just weekdays. If you allow yourself to sleep in and wake up at a different time on weekends, you're just going to mess up your sleep schedule and make it harder for that habit to stick. You'll know it's become normal when you start waking up before your alarm goes off. And when your feet hit the floor, that's a win because that keystone habit has been completed.

For those first hundred days, don't force yourself to do a lot of new activities, but you'll have some free time, so you might as well do something with it. Maybe read one day. The next day, you might do some yoga. The day after that, you might feel like journaling. Or go for a run. Or catch up on some work. Or meditate. The only thing you focused on accomplishing was getting up early, but look how much more you can get done. Waking up early turned into extra reading, yoga, journaling, and running. That's what makes a keystone habit so effective. One good thing begets many more good things, which you're more likely to continue, making them habits too.

After those one hundred days, or when waking up early has become a habit that you don't have to think about, move on to your next keystone habit. Maybe you want to start working out, so plan to do something physical every day for the next one hundred days.

That might involve going to the gym a couple of days a week, doing yoga a couple of days, walking around the block perhaps while listening to an audiobook, or just getting up and moving your body on some days. That's all you focus on for the next one hundred days. Start doing that, and it might make you want to eat a little healthier. Then you start drinking more water and getting to bed earlier, so your body can recover better. You then cut back on how much alcohol you drink. All you did was focus on that one habit of working out daily for one hundred days, and it led to going to the gym, doing yoga, eating healthier, drinking more water, and going to bed early.

After that next hundred days, and your workout routine has also become a habit, turn your attention to the next keystone habit. If you focus on one thing at a time for one hundred days, you will have developed at least three powerful keystone habits over a year. That's more than enough to positively influence you and get you moving in the direction you want to go. It can also change your life forever.

Habit Stacking

Another method for creating habits that stick is called habit stacking, which was popularized by the social scientist and author B. J. Fogg through his Tiny Habits method. The idea is simple: Attach a new habit to the back end of an existing habit. After I do [old habit], I will do [new habit].

Maybe you want to start practicing affirmations every day but have trouble doing it consistently. Rather than carving out time in your schedule to say affirmations, do it right after you perform another habit—like brushing your teeth. So, every time you brush your teeth, you say your affirmations immediately after. You're already in the habit of brushing your teeth; the brain does it on autopilot, so you make it easy on yourself by attaching the new action to the back end of a habit. Which eventually becomes a habit. That's why it's called habit stacking.

This can work with almost anything. Here are some examples that might work for you: After you sit down at your desk to work, drink a glass of water. After you greet your partner when they get home from work, tell them how much you appreciate them. After you turn off the light to sleep at night, think of one thing you're grateful for. After you take your first bite of food, consider how grateful you are for another meal. After you return home from work, put away your cell phone and play with your kids. After you make your morning coffee, do fifty push-ups.

This works because your existing behavior or habit triggers that next action. Pretty soon, you won't have to work to do the second action because it's become a habit that you do on autopilot. Fogg developed what he calls the ABC of tiny habits, which is a process that helps make a new habit stick:

A. Anchor
B. Behavior
C. Celebration

The *anchor* is the old habit (what you already do), that reminds you to perform the *behavior* (the new habit), and then you make sure to *celebrate* when it's completed. The third part, the celebration, is super important. It doesn't have to be big. It can be a mini-celebration you do in your head. Something as simple as telling yourself "Hell, yeah!" or "Good job!" is often all you need to appreciate that accomplishment. If it fits your personality, try doing a little dance. We'll get into the science of why this is important in a later chapter but get in the habit of rewarding yourself and celebrating your accomplishments.

Set Your New Standard

Every personal development podcast and self-help book talks about habits, but there is something more important than habits that very few people discuss: standards. And if properly utilized, standards will help you stick to your habits. Habits are the children of standards because if you have standards, you will naturally create habits.

In their simplest form, standards are what you deem to be acceptable and unacceptable. Standards are directly linked to your identity, and they determine the levels you won't drop below. Just like the thermostat sets the temperature comfort zone in your house, your standards set your personal comfort zone. Look at your body. There is a good chance that you've been in the same basic shape for the past five or maybe even ten years. Why? Because you hold yourself to a certain standard. It might also be the reason why most people aren't able to significantly improve their physique. That's a standard, too.

What about your bank account? Chances are that you've been hovering around the same amount for years. If you're used to seeing $5,000, that's become your standard, so if you have some major expenses and your account drops to $3,000, you will tighten the belt, not spend as much, and save until you get your account back to where you feel safe and comfortable. The opposite is true as well. Let's say you get a $2,000 raise or a bonus and you find your account balloons to $7,000. You might go out more often and buy yourself a few things you normally wouldn't. It doesn't happen all at once, but eventually you find yourself right back at $5,000. Why? Because that's your comfort zone. It's seventy-two degrees on the thermostat. You aren't used to or comfortable with having less money in your account, and unfortunately you aren't used to having more either, so you find a way to get back to where you're most comfortable.

The standards you hold yourself to have essentially created the life you currently have. Everything from your friendships and relationships to the cleanliness of your home comes down to your standards. Think of your standards as the ground floor that you will not drop below. There are always levels above that ground floor, but to get there, you have to raise your standards. If you aren't where you want to be, you won't be able to grow and create that amazing life unless you learn how to hold yourself to a higher standard.

Not properly adjusting your standards now will prevent you from taking the action necessary to follow through on your habits later. For example, one of the habits you might want to develop is waking up earlier. It's a great habit that most highly successful people share, but if you don't have the standard of prioritizing your sleep, which involves getting ready the night before, going to bed earlier, and making sure that you get a good night's rest, it's going to be difficult to implement that habit and wake up when the alarm goes off in the morning. If you don't prioritize your sleep, the alarm will go off early, and you will struggle to get out of bed. Why? Because you haven't set that standard. You need to set the standard first because standards are what allow you to follow through on developing habits.

Think of it like this: You aren't going to suddenly stop paying your bills, not show up for work, neglect your responsibilities, and go live on the street. Why? Because it's below your standards, so it's not an option. But when the alarm goes off early in the morning, you struggle to get up and hit snooze every once in a while. Why? Because you set that standard.

What if you made living on the street and hitting snooze mental equivalents? You'd think, *No way on earth am I ever going to hit that snooze button!* It sounds drastic, but you can see what I mean.

Let's say that one of your goals is to lose fifteen pounds and get down to 10 percent body fat. I know some people who work out twice a day, so it will probably be easy for them to create the habits needed to reach that goal. I know other people who haven't worked out in years, so it will be much more difficult because they haven't set that standard.

Reaching that weight goal requires exercising and eating healthy foods, which you will have to make habits, but if you're used to eating junk food and fast food, you haven't set that standard yet, so it will be much more difficult for you to adapt. I'll bet that if you accidentally dropped your food onto the pavement of a disgusting parking lot, you wouldn't pick it up and eat it. But you have no problem eating junk food and fast food even though it's not healthy and makes you feel bad. That's because you've set those standards. What if your standard was to make eating fast food and junk food the mental equivalent of eating food off the pavement? You would never consider touching the stuff because it's below your standards. If you want to change your body, you need to change your standards.

You live and die by your standards. They have created the life you have now, but they won't give you the life you want. If you want to reach your true potential, you need to change your standards before you begin to think about habits.

During my interview with Jeff Hoffman on my podcast, he told me he was close friends with former boxing heavyweight champion

Evander Holyfield. Jeff wasn't the same caliber of athlete as Holyfield, but one day Jeff watched him do this insane workout that was also very precise because it involved exactly three hundred sets. One of those sets would be hard for a normal human being, but Jeff was tasked with counting while Evander did three hundred. At the end, Holyfield asked Jeff, "Was that 299 or was it 300?"

"I think it was 300," Jeff said.

"Jeff, was it 299 or was it 300?"

"I think it was 300. What does it matter?"

Holyfield said, "The difference between 300 and 299 is the difference between the heavyweight champion of the world and every other fighter out there."

He then did one more set to make sure he completed three hundred. The reason he was the champ was because he always held himself to a higher standard, and that involved completing what he set out to do.

If you want to achieve greatness and become something special, you have to put in 100 percent and not allow yourself to come up short. That starts with the standards you set because they create personal expectations that you must live up to. If you want to take that a step further, take a page from Evander Holyfield's playbook and utilize a standard that you can track or record so you can see whether you're succeeding or slacking off. This is a simple way to get out of your own head and put those standards to the test in the real world.

Keep in mind that much of what we've discussed throughout this book is connected, and standards are no exception because they are directly linked to your identity and your goals. When you become a new character and change your identity, make sure you set new standards for that identity. When you set a goal to lose a certain amount of weight or make a certain amount of money, you don't just set the goal; you must become the person whose healthy habits will lead to your achieving that goal by setting that standard for yourself. This takes willpower out of the equation and makes your healthy habits automatic.

Standards bleed into each other. When we're slipping in one area of life, we're often slipping in another, and this can be traced back to our standards. The opposite is true as well. Once we begin raising our standards in one area, it becomes easier to raise them in another. Change starts from the top down, and it begins by holding ourselves to a higher standard.

* * *

Consistency and hard work are required to achieve your goals because your future success will be the culmination of all the micro-actions you take every day. You don't have to fight an uphill battle, and you don't have to force yourself to complete a laundry list of positive things every day. The trick is learning how to make those micro-actions habits, and eventually raise your standards, so you can take advantage of the brain's natural tendency to create shortcuts and conserve energy. It all starts with doing an audit to identify your own behaviors and habits. Look for ways to replace negative habits with new, positive ones formed by habit stacking, but keep it simple. Don't shoot for the moon. Start by incorporating one keystone habit into your life. Stick to that for one hundred days and watch the positive ripple effect it will have in all areas of your life.

Journal Prompts

- What habits do you currently have that bring you closer to your goals?

- What habits do you currently have that are taking you further away from your goals?

- What can you do to make it easier on yourself to eliminate bad habits and create good ones?

- What is one keystone habit that could potentially make the biggest difference in your life if you implemented it today?

- What habits can you begin stacking throughout your day?

For more journal prompts and video lessons from this book, go to: https://RobDial.com/LevelUp.

CHAPTER 11

Neuroplasticity

The Science of Changing Your Brain

If you've been in a London taxicab, you might have noticed how the drivers don't rely on maps or GPS. That's not by accident. It dates back to a law created in 1865 for horse-drawn carriages, and for some reason, the law still prevents taxicab drivers from relying on maps. All taxi drivers must pass an intricate test known as "The Knowledge" to get their green badge. That means drivers must memorize every street and know their way around the city much better than the average driver. Given that London has twenty-five thousand crisscrossing streets that are anything but an easy-to-remember grid, it's no surprise that it takes some drivers four years to master the area and that half of applicants fail the test.

Neuroscientists studied the impact this had on those drivers' brains.[1] They followed seventy-nine aspiring taxi drivers for four years as they prepared for the test. At the beginning of the study, the researchers performed MRIs and found that all the aspiring drivers had about the same size hippocampus—the part of the brain that deals with the kind of memory needed for navigation. After four years, thirty-nine of the drivers had passed The Knowledge test. A second MRI was done on all seventy-nine study participants, and the hippocampi in the brains of the ones who had passed the test were larger than those of the other participants. During those four years, the brains of those London taxicab drivers literally had changed.

This isn't a unique phenomenon. People who are blind and read Braille develop the area of the brain that is receptive to the sense of touch, so it grows in size over time; but because of the way they use their hands, new connections are created in the brain that reorganize and change its structure. Your brain does this without your realizing it, for instance within the regions of the brain that control your dominant hand. Those regions are stronger structurally and have different connections than the regions that control your non-dominant hand.

What's so beautiful about the brain is that you can mold and change it through repeated action. The term neuroplasticity means the brain's ability to form and reorganize synaptic connections, especially in response to learning or experience. This means that you can change your brain whenever you want, so all those needle-moving activities and healthy habits that you want to implement to achieve your goals can be done on autopilot.

> What's so beautiful about the brain is that you can mold and change it through repeated action.

Neuroplasticity takes three forms: passive plasticity, maladaptive plasticity, and adaptive plasticity.

Passive Plasticity

There is no getting around the fact that it is much easier to change your brain when you're young. The first time you go to the beach, the first movie you watch in a theater, or the first time you go to a professional baseball game can all change the brain through what's called passive plasticity. The change doesn't require intention; it just happens. At a young age, your brain is designed for plasticity. It wants to grow.

Tiger Woods started playing golf before the age of two. Floyd Mayweather learned to box at seven. That doesn't mean they automatically became champions because they started at a young age, but it is safe to say they wouldn't have experienced nearly the same success had they tried to learn their respective sports later in life. A child's brain can be shaped in a way that an adult's cannot. That's why kids can pick up a new language much easier than adults.

Our brains have billions of cells that are called neurons. The electrical activity of these neurons dictates our experiences by transferring chemical signals between cells after information has been received from the outside world. This triggers a series of actions and reactions.

Dr. Carla Shatz famously said "neurons that fire together wire together" to describe the nervous system's ability to change in response to experience.[2] This means that the more you do something, the more it changes the wiring of your brain. The neurons you use become stronger and the ones you don't use become weaker, but after roughly the age of twenty-five, these communication lanes close, and the synapses, or space between the neurons, begin to shrink, making it more difficult for the brain to make these passive changes. It's still possible to change your brain—it just requires more attention and repetition.

Maladaptive Plasticity

The second way your brain can change is through maladaptive plasticity, which involves the experience of traumatic events. The brain releases chemicals to become hyperalert as a defense mechanism during a life-and-death situation. It can even feel like time slows down (called tachypsychia). A friend of mine was in an accident that caused his car to roll over a few times, and he told me that he could see the glass moving in front of his face as if it were in slow motion.

There is an evolutionary reason for this response. Our ancient ancestors had to learn how to survive in their environments. Picture living a hundred thousand years ago, and you're walking along a large body of water with a companion. Suddenly, an alligator heaves out of the water and snatches away your friend, who is never seen again. That traumatic event releases massive amounts of epinephrine and acetylcholine to make you focused and alert so you can survive. The epinephrine creates alertness, and the acetylcholine acts as a highlighter to mark the neurons that are active during that experience so that the brain can protect you in the future. The next time you approach any body of water, you might associate it with danger because your brain has been "rewired." These are the same chemicals that are released when you're starting to focus, which is why it can seem stressful.

This is precisely how post-traumatic stress disorder (PTSD) works. A traumatic event can change the wiring of the brain and the way you interpret certain experiences. After being in a bad car accident, for instance, you might become hesitant when returning to that same area or anticipate a scenario similar to the circumstances under which the accident occurred. It's the brain's way of creating red flags to help you become alert to potential danger.

Over time, you might be able to disassociate the difficult emotions from the tragic event, but you will never forget the actual event. You will even remember the moments leading up to that event. You might remember the entire day. This is why some people might be triggered by an event that seems ordinary. It's not that they are reminded of the trauma; they are reminded of one of the events leading up to it. And because this memory is also encoded in the amygdala, it can illicit an emotional reaction that makes PTSD difficult to treat.[3] This shows that with enough emotion and focus, the brain can change because of a single event.

Adaptive Plasticity

Passive and maladaptive plasticity are ways our brains can change because of factors outside of our control. Adaptive plasticity is the type of neuroplasticity that we can influence. It starts by doing what we discussed in the previous chapter—performing an action repeatedly until it becomes a habit. This eventually changes the brain.

The brain will resist change and try to revert back to well-worn paths it is used to because that requires less energy, so change will take time. You can't do something today and expect your brain to be different tomorrow. As the saying goes, "Repetition is the mother of skill." That's what it takes to build up myelin and change the wiring of your brain. What's myelin? It's a sheath along nerves that allows the signals in your brain to be sent more efficiently and without disruption. Picture a cord going into an electrical outlet, like the one on your laptop. It's rubber on the outside, but that rubber protects the copper wire on the inside that sends the signal. Myelin is like the rubber insulating the cord. More repetition creates more myelin, allowing the signal to be sent faster and more efficiently.[4]

The brain undergoes a three-step process over time to support learning, build up myelin, and create new pathways. It first changes chemically, then structurally, and finally functionally.[5]

1. Chemical Change

Depending on your thoughts, your brain can increase or decrease the chemicals it sends to neurons. This can improve short-term memory and help you learn a new skill.

Let's say that you want to learn to play the piano, and on your first day, you learn "Mary Had a Little Lamb." You had never played it before, but you made a huge improvement in a short amount of time when learning to play this simple song. That's your brain sending more chemicals to the neurons, but what happens the next day? You might not be able to play the song that seemed so easy the day before. It feels like you forgot everything you learned. Several factors contribute to how and why memories "stick" (sleep, focus, level of emotional stress, fatigue, etc.), but one reason why the song didn't stay with you was because your brain increased the chemical signaling between neurons to improve only your short-term memory. It's like writing a message in the sand on a beach that is soon washed away by waves. If you want to make a more significant and permanent change to your brain, you must go deeper. You have to change the structure of your brain.

2. Structural Change

It takes time, effort, and repetition to create long-term memory or improve motor skills. When you do something repeatedly, chemical changes lead to structural changes, which is why it's so important to keep showing up and working day after day because that process of learning creates brand-new connections between neurons that weren't there before. You're literally changing the physical structure of your brain. It doesn't matter what you're doing; when you learn and focus on something repeatedly for an extended period, it can eventually change the structure of your brain, no matter how old you are.

Chemical changes to the brain are like water that builds up or runs down a landscape after it rains. Over time, the rain or accumulation of water can forge new paths that change the landscape permanently. Given enough time, those changes can be monumental—like the Grand Canyon, formed by the Colorado River cutting through rock over time. Structural changes can get different sections of the brain working together for the first time. This is what happens with London taxicab drivers and people who learn how to read Braille.

3. Functional Change

After the structure of the brain changes, what makes those changes last in the long term is when you change the actual function of your brain. When you are learning something, entire networks of brain activity shift, so the action you're learning becomes easier over time and requires less effort. You don't have to think about it anymore, and that's how you know you're changing the function of your brain.

One of the best examples of this occurs in piano players. To play the piano, both hands work independently. There are eighty-eight keys, and you can play up to ten notes at a time, which is more demanding than some other instruments. When learning to play the piano, people must overcome being either right-handed or left-handed, so over time, the dexterity of their weaker hand matches that of their dominant hand. Even more impressive than that is how they develop a unique brain capacity that improves the way their brain functions.

Researchers have scanned the brains of pianists when they are playing and found that their brains pump less blood to the regions associated with fine motor skills when compared with the average person's brain.[6] This means the brain doesn't have to expend as much energy to concentrate. The pianists weren't born that way; their brains developed over time with practice.

Another researcher discovered that experienced jazz pianists, while improvising, created different connections in the frontal lobe of their brains compared with those who didn't play the piano. This part of the brain is responsible for problem-solving, decision-making, and also spontaneity, which meant these pianists could turn off the part of the brain that would automatically provide a stereotypical response. That allowed them to play in a way that was a true representation of who they were and not copy someone else.[7]

When you change the function of the brain, actions become automatic, such as driving home from work or turning off the lights when you leave a room. That song you forgot how to play on day two will be something you can play on autopilot without thinking about it, but there is a catch.

If at least 47 percent of your daily actions are habitual, then nearly half of what you do is repetitive. If almost half of what you do every day is the same as what you did the day before, do you really think your brain will change? The brain always tries to move back to a state of homeostasis, so to change your brain, you need to change your actions and then do those same actions over and over. New learning creates new neural pathways. Consistency is key, so show up every day.

Neuroplasticity can also help you change your thoughts. There is some science behind the power of positive thinking because it can activate parts of the brain associated with self-processing and reward.[8] Positive thinking and optimism can decrease stress and lower cortisol levels.[9] Positivity has even been shown to improve cardiovascular health and reduce other health risks.[10] The trick is learning how to make it a habit.

As a former pessimist, I understand how difficult it can be to change your thinking when you've become so used to looking at the world through a negative lens. While it's true that you may not be able to control your first thought, you can control your second thought. So if you can get in the habit of disrupting that pattern when you recognize that first negative thought by making sure your second thought is positive, you will strengthen those pathways. It's a process that will take some work, but here are three simple ways you can begin to make this change.

1. Practice gratitude. Incorporate this practice into your morning or nighttime routine.
2. Create positive affirmations. When you create an affirmation, it should meet three criteria: it needs to be true, present tense, and empowering. So instead of saying something like "Money is flowing to me from all areas of the universe," say something like "I am capable of creating the life I want." Write an affirmation on sticky notes that you can place throughout your home or set it as the background of your phone. You can even make it a habit to say

affirmations every morning in the shower, or set an alarm with a reminder if you're having trouble getting the habit to stick.

3. Don't forget about your environment. You want to make sure your environment is conducive to positive thoughts. That includes the people you invite into it, who you follow on social media, and the type of content you consume. If you spend the night watching murder mysteries with a group of miserable friends, it's going to be much harder to stay positive.

Over time, this will help that first negative thought grow weaker and make it easier for you to make that second thought positive. Do it enough and positive thinking will become more natural and eventually effortless. It's not a cure-all for mental health issues, but positive thoughts will help you shape a more positive brain.

Whether you want to change your thoughts or your actions, deliberate practice is essential. It's not about sitting down and playing the same guitar solo you've been playing forever. It's about sitting down and trying to play something that's challenging and outside your comfort zone. You must direct that change and make a conscious effort to improve on something. None of this change can occur by accident. You aren't a kid anymore. You've seen and done a lot. Your brain is set in many of its ways. You absolutely must WANT to change to rewire your brain. Lara Boyd, a brain researcher at the University of British Columbia, reinforced this during her Ted Talk titled "After Watching This, Your Brain Will Not Be the Same" when she said: "the primary driver of change in your brain is your behavior, so there is no neuroplasticity drug you can take. Nothing is more effective than practice at helping you learn and the bottom line is you have to do the work."[11] This bears repeating: Nothing is more effective than practice and repetition to help you learn. You must do the work, and it's not going to be easy.

Embrace the Struggle

Everyone learns differently. Some kids thrive in traditional schools, and others don't. Some people can learn an instrument quickly, while others more easily develop the motor skills required to play a sport. Some of the things that are easy for you might be difficult for me. You have to figure out the best way you learn, but one essential part of the process is making mistakes. You must struggle to learn. That's how the brain changes.

When you experience something difficult and you get agitated, that's a good thing because it's a sign your brain is releasing the two primary chemicals essential for it to change: acetylcholine and epinephrine. Acetylcholine is like a spotlight in the brain that helps you focus. Epinephrine is another name for the adrenaline in your brain. These are the same chemicals released when you experience a traumatic event, and they are also released when you are trying to learn something. Your brain undergoes a similar process to trigger neuroplasticity. The trick is that you must push through the discomfort.

Most people get so agitated that they assume what they're trying to do is hopeless, so they give up and quit. They don't realize they are stopping at the most crucial time because the brain is about to change. The greater the struggle, the greater the transformation in your brain, so lean into it. Let your mantra be *If it doesn't challenge me, it doesn't change me*. From this point forward, try to think differently about that agitation and frustration. Instead of feeling discouraged, get encouraged because you know that your brain is about to change. You just have to stick with it.

> If it doesn't challenge you, it doesn't change you.

For example, what happens if you go to the gym, get on a couple of machines, and do just what feels easy. And you keep doing those same exercises over and over. However often you go to the gym, you won't get the body you want. Why? Because you aren't pushing yourself. If you want to build muscle, lose fat, and get in better shape, you must lift heavier and train harder progressively. The brain and body are made to adapt.

Most people understand that about the body, but not as many realize that the brain works the same way. It likes its patterns, so when you try to rewrite them, there will be resistance. You must push through and past your limits to grow. Once again, if it doesn't challenge you, it doesn't change you. Once you start to step out of your comfort zone to do new and different things, you'll probably find that you aren't that good at them. Let's be honest: you might be terrible. I've been playing guitar for fifteen years, and some songs I've been playing so long that I can play them in my sleep; but when I try to learn a new song, it sounds like I just picked up a guitar for the first time. It's pretty bad. I get frustrated when I keep making mistakes, so I want to go back to playing the easy stuff. I didn't realize for a long time that it was good to make mistakes! That's the first part of the equation, but there is another equally important component that you can't skip if you want to change your brain.

Sleep: When the Real Change Occurs

It doesn't matter whether you're studying for a test, trying to learn a new song on the piano, or watching your caveperson friend get snatched away by an alligator; the brain doesn't change right at that moment. What happens in the moment is the epinephrine and acetylcholine mark the neurons that need to be changed because of that event. The actual change occurs when we sleep because that's when the brain reorganizes those neurons and synapses. That's the final step.

Let's go back to the workout analogy because the way the brain and body change tend to be so similar. Think of how important recovery is after a workout to build muscle and improve performance. It doesn't matter how tough, determined, or fit you are; the human body can be pushed only so far before its nutrients are depleted. The workout process breaks down muscle, and it's through nutrition and sleep that it builds back up stronger. The brain works the same way. Change doesn't only happen during the attempt to learn; it happens when you sleep.

The hippocampus is the part of your brain responsible for learning and storing memory. It takes what you do and learn throughout the day, stores it, and rebroadcasts those memories while you sleep to rewire the brain. This process is called memory consolidation. It helps you solve your complex challenges throughout the day and is another reason why sleep is so important.[12]

While sleep allows the hippocampus to store and learn what it experienced, something similar occurs when you take a break, as you do during those five minutes in between sessions of the Pomodoro Technique. It's called hippocampal replay, and it's not as effective as sleep, but (combined with the repetition of performing the Pomodoro

Technique over time) it helps you to store what you've learned in the brain to accelerate neuroplasticity and let those changes sink in.[13] And you don't want to get on your phone during rest periods while learning or doing deep, focused work because that can diminish any restorative impact of restful activity.

What's More Important: Talent or Skill?

What makes an incredible musician or athlete great is not that they are more talented than everyone else; it's that they've developed their skills through practice, which changed the way their brain functions. Through extended practice periods, musicians train their muscles to improve the brain-body connection. Their ear for the notes becomes fine-tuned. Yes, some people have more genuine talent, and playing music comes easier to them than others, but to truly succeed and be great, you don't want to rely on talent—you want to become skilled. And the only way to do that is through intense, prolonged practice.

One of my favorite sayings is "Hard work beats talent when talent doesn't work hard." You can see this concept play out with pro athletes. There are many stories of phenoms coming out of high school and college who are predicted to set the league on fire when they get to the pros because they have such incredible talent. Quarterbacks JaMarcus Russell and Ryan Leaf were highly touted and received contracts worth millions of dollars, but they both flamed out, never lived up to their potential, and became known as two of the biggest busts in NFL history. Compare them to Tom Brady, who was selected in the sixth round as the 199th pick. Six quarterbacks were selected before him. Nobody expected much of anything from Brady, but he went on to set all-time NFL records in completions, passing yards, and touchdown passes, while winning more Super Bowls than any player in NFL history. But why do some phenoms never live up to their potential while other overlooked athletes become superstars?

> "Hard work beats talent when talent doesn't work hard."

Sure, there are a lot of outside factors when it comes to sports, but the difference between talent and skill plays a huge role. Talent is an innate ability. It's an excellent advantage to have and can get you very far, much like positive thinking and wanting great things to happen in life. But if you genuinely want to live up to your potential and achieve your goals, you need skill. That requires practice, hard work, and taking action. And just like there are plenty of athletes who had the talent but never developed their skill, there are plenty of underdog stories about players who were unknown or came from small colleges to become stars. Very few people heard of Tom Brady when he was just out of college. He wasn't the most athletic or talented player, but he is living proof that hard work beats talent when talent doesn't work hard.

The beautiful thing about being a human being is that we can develop any skill we want if we are willing to put in the time and effort. With enough hard work, you can literally build yourself up and become almost anyone you want. How amazing is that?

Mixed martial arts champion Conor McGregor is quoted as saying: "There's no talent here, this is hard work. This is an obsession. Talent does not exist; we are all equals as human beings. You could be anyone if you put in the time. You will reach the top, and that's that. I am not talented. I am obsessed." I'd go so far as to say that calling someone talented who honed their craft through hard work undermines those years of hard work.

This type of change is driven by behavior, specifically, deliberate practice over an extended period. Your brain first changes chemically in the short term, structurally in the intermediate term after extended practice, and functionally in the long term once the action becomes second nature. That's why you can't become really good at the piano overnight. But because of neuroplasticity, you can learn almost anything in time and make it become a reflexive habit that you do automatically.

Journal Prompts

- What have you done in the past that may have contributed to structural changes in your brain? These could be intentional changes (going to school, pursuing a hobby) or unintentional (a traumatic experience or even a bad habit you've fallen into).

- Pick one of your top goals. How can you use daily deliberate practice to create structural changes in your brain?

- What skills do you need to develop or dedicate more time to cultivating to achieve that goal?

- What process will you put in place to accomplish that?

For more journal prompts and video lessons from this book, go to:
https://RobDial.com/LevelUp.

CHAPTER 12

Creating a Dopamine Reward System

Falling in Love with the Process

Kobe Bryant was an eighteen-time All-Star and won five NBA championships. From a very young age, he set out to become one of the best players who ever set foot on a basketball court, but many argue that it wasn't winning that he loved the most.

Bryant knew that to be the best he had to practice and train as much as possible. By getting up to practice at 4 a.m. every day, he could get in much more practice time than the average player who would wake up around 9 or 10 a.m. He loved knowing that he was working hard while his competition was asleep. It gave him a sense of pride to know that nobody else was willing to put in the amount of work that he was because he knew that if he took those same micro-actions day after day, week after week, and year after year, his competition would never be able to catch up to or match the amount of work he put into improving his game. Even after winning one of those championships, Bryant was back at the gym the very next morning because, more than anything else, he loved the process of trying to become the best. His trainer, Tim Grover, said the most challenging thing about working with Kobe Bryant was trying to get him to stop.

University of Alabama football coach Nick Saban has been so successful that his team has been ranked number one at some point during the season for thirteen straight years. Part of his coaching method involves not having his team focus on the championship at the end of the season, but instead having them focus on each individual play of the game. If players give everything they have and execute each play to the best of their abilities, they will get to where they want to go. Neither Bryant nor Saban might have consciously realized it, but what they were doing was creating a dopamine reward system and attaching it to their training process. In doing so, Bryant and Saban's players were *falling in love* with the hard work they were doing.

I've spoken to and worked with many driven people who have the attitude that they aren't going to enjoy or reward themselves until they reach their goals. They don't want to celebrate until they get to the finish line. This is common, but it's the opposite of what you want to do when trying to take continuous action over time. You might be able to push yourself to reach your goal through brute force, but eventually, even the best of us will run out of steam because that's a long time to go without a reward. And without a reward in place, it's significantly more challenging to keep going when you face obstacles, so this type of brute force often leads to burnout.

You've probably heard the saying "It's the journey and not the destination," or "The person who loves walking will walk farther than the person who loves the destination." These may be clichés, but clichés are clichés for a reason—because they are true. The point is that if you fall in love with the journey, the results will come. That's the idea behind action-based goals that focus on the process, and not results-based goals that focus on the outcome.

The true secret to achieving your goal is not to celebrate when you accomplish it but to find ways to celebrate the process by creating a reward around the completion of your action-based goals. In the same way that micro-actions over time add up to big results, celebrating action-based goals along the way makes you love the process, creates motivation to keep going, and helps you push further than you would if you waited until the end.

> The true secret to achieving your goal is not to celebrate when you accomplish it but to find ways to celebrate the process.

Most important, action-based goals help you fall in love with the process, so you don't have to force yourself to change your brain. You'll want to, thanks to dopamine.

It's All About Dopamine

Many people clump dopamine together with serotonin and think of them both as feel-good chemicals, but that's inaccurate. Serotonin is an internally focused chemical that creates a sense of peace and calm while helping you to feel grateful. Dopamine is an externally focused chemical. It's the chemical of motivation, craving, and wanting more. It increases alertness and readiness and is linked to reward.

When you feel lazy and unmotivated, you are in what's called a low-dopamine state. When you are excited and motivated, that's a high-dopamine state. Dopamine drives you closer to your goals, and it's one of the main chemicals responsible for keeping our species alive and thriving because it's one of the primary chemicals involved in hunting and gathering. Think about going on a hunt and tracking an animal that you know will feed your entire tribe. There's a dopamine release in that anticipation. When you spot the animal, there's another dopamine release, and another when you kill the animal and another when you bring it home and are celebrated by the tribe.

We don't have to hunt our own food to survive anymore, but we still release dopamine when we're excited or celebrating, and since it's externally focused, it propels us forward, and we become motivated to seek out more. Think about any athletic event when one of the teams made a miraculous comeback to squeak out a last-second victory. Players for both of those teams expended the same amount of energy. They played the same game for the same amount of time, but which team has more energy after the game? The players on the team that won stay up all night and celebrate. The team that lost? Not so much. They're exhausted. They're drained because they didn't receive the dopamine lift that came with winning.

What makes taking consistent action and turning those actions into habits so difficult is that it's hard to keep this pace up for an extended period. Even though it's healthy to fail at the chemical level since that's how we learn, there is no positive reward in that. When you feel stress and frustration trying to do something new, there is no natural reason why dopamine is released. Your happiness, motivation, and drive will all be determined by outside factors, making it much more difficult to succeed because eventually, without that reward, the grind will wear you down. It doesn't matter how much willpower you have. That's why so many people quit when things get tough. But it doesn't have to be that way. Epinephrine may be what first gives us the fuel to put in the effort, but dopamine is what refills our tanks.

We may not realize it, but we are all dopamine addicts because it can be released in many different ways. Watching television can be a dopamine rush. Scrolling through social media can be a dopamine rush. Being able to buy anything you want on Amazon with the click of a button and having it delivered to your door the next day is a dopamine rush. And while being addicted to dopamine in these ways can prevent us from taking action toward our goals, when properly channeled, dopamine is extremely powerful. It can help remove the extra friction you encounter by providing motivation; but arguably what makes dopamine so unique is that you have a say in when it's released.

During my interview on my podcast with Andrew Huberman, he talked extensively about how dopamine is also a subjective molecule. Human beings are clever creatures. One reason why we are at the top of the food chain is that we have learned how to control our own dopamine process. The things that I want more of and that create a feeling of reward for me might not be the same as they are for you, and so we might have two different ways of going about releasing dopamine. There are limitations: you aren't going to release dopamine by telling yourself you love to work out when you hate it, but you can control dopamine release by celebrating yourself for showing up when you didn't want to. That will make it more likely you show up tomorrow to work out again.

What Is a Dopamine Reward?

When you experience pleasure in response to stimuli, that's dopamine being released. That dopamine signals to the brain that the behavior will be rewarded with pleasure, which motivates you to repeat that behavior. This occurs naturally, but when you understand how this process works, you can manufacture this response and use dopamine to your advantage.

The "celebration" part of B. J. Fogg's ABC process (see Chapter 10) can be as simple as saying, "You're doing great!" "Keep at it!" "I'm taking the action I didn't want to take earlier in the day, and I'm proud of myself!" That's it! Even that small celebration sends a hit of dopamine to your brain, and you will feel good, accomplished, and motivated. That's the dopamine reward, but the trick is that you must really celebrate and FEEL that sense of accomplishment. You can't fake it or merely go through the motions.

Words are very powerful because when you say (or even think) certain words, you can't help but feel something. So, if you are positively celebrating progress, you will feel good. And if you talk down to yourself, you will make yourself feel bad. Talking down to yourself might be the best way to demotivate yourself and make it harder to achieve what you're working toward. This is why the story we tell ourselves and the words we use to tell that story matter so much. Talking down to yourself as a form of motivation can backfire if it makes you feel bad, and it's much harder to take action when you feel bad. It's natural for us to resist things we don't like and move toward things we do like. Talking yourself up can be all you need to flip that little switch in your brain to release just enough dopamine to motivate you to keep going, so be very careful about the words you use.

Back when I worked at my sales job, we often tried to make one hundred calls every single day, and for those of you who have worked in sales, you know that can be torture. One of my mentors told me how I could make that process just a little bit easier. He told me to sit down at the phone with a bag of Skittles (because I love Skittles), and every time I made ten phone calls, I could have three Skittles. That's it. Just three. I was rewarding myself after every ten phone calls, which kept me going. And when I got to the end and completed all one hundred calls, I could finish the rest of the bag. The key was rewarding the action, not the end result. I didn't realize it at the time, but I was creating a dopamine reward system.

Just like in the movie *E.T.* when the kids lure E.T. with a trail of Reese's Pieces, the dopamine reward system is the trail of candies you're creating for yourself that will lead you toward your goal and, ultimately, success. This is more than a metaphor: chocolate actually can increase dopamine levels; so having a tiny piece of chocolate after a workout can make it more likely you will show up the next day, however counterproductive that seems, simply because your body and brain want the dopamine. I still do this today, but I've found other ways to celebrate that don't involve candy. When I finish recording an episode of my podcast, I think about all of the people that episode could help, and say to myself, "Hell, yeah! That was a great episode. Good job!" And I really FEEL it. That mini-celebration makes me feel excited and accomplished. More important, it releases dopamine, and since it's attached to the process, not the end result, I become more driven to record the next episode. Today, when I think of my podcast, I'm focused on getting each episode done, not becoming one of the top one hundred podcasters or getting millions of downloads. That's part of the reason why I've been able to record more than thirteen hundred episodes in the past seven years, while the average podcaster quits after only seven episodes. It was never about becoming the biggest podcast; it was about making each episode the best it could be because I knew each one could have a positive impact on someone's life.

Celebrating yourself is a crucial step when creating a dopamine reward system, but it's also a great way to help you feel better. We pay attention to the negative much too often and beat ourselves up constantly. Instead, we should get in the habit of ignoring the bad and praising the good. We should get in the habit of celebrating ourselves when we do something difficult or make progress. Think of how excited a parent gets when watching their child get a hit in T-ball. Rarely will anybody celebrate themselves as they would a loved one, yet it can have such a positive impact on your life. There are many creative ways you can go about celebrating and motivating yourself throughout the day.

Former Navy SEAL and elite endurance athlete David Goggins utilizes something that he calls "the mental cookie jar" in his mind when he's on long runs. If there is ever a moment when he begins to doubt himself, questions whether he'll be able to finish, or feels like giving up, he reaches into his mental cookie jar, which is full of reminders of his accomplishments. Just by reminding himself of everything he's already done, he's telling himself how great he is, which is a dopamine reward system that motivates him to keep going.

When I interviewed former Navy SEAL Rich Diviney, he told me that when he was going through Hell Week of the Basic Underwater Demolition/SEAL (BUD/S) training, which is designed to break people, he knew that the people who laughed and made jokes would almost always make it. They probably didn't realize it, but it turns out that laughing can lower your adrenaline and release dopamine, so you never hit that threshold that forces your body to shut down or give up. If you're out on a long run or want to work out longer and harder while preventing yourself from hitting a wall, make yourself laugh. It can't be a fake laugh. It has to be a genuine laugh, which will cause your brain to release dopamine that will allow you to push through because it serves as a buffer against adrenaline and cortisol.

Think about a time when you felt absolutely miserable and then someone made a joke that completely changed your mood and possibly your day. Laughing gives us more energy and makes us feel like things aren't so bad after all. The therapeutic benefits of laughter have been studied.[1] It's a great feeling that comes complete with a sense of accomplishment. The next time you feel stressed out or hit a wall during the day, take five minutes to watch a video of your favorite comedian because laughing will create a dopamine reward system that can lower your adrenaline and allow you to keep going.

There are many other ways you can increase dopamine naturally, including exercise, which can increase dopamine up to two times, and a cold plunge (at a safe temperature), which as we saw earlier, can increase dopamine 2.5 times. Dopamine will remain in your system after a cold plunge for up to three hours before returning to the normal baseline.[2]

The Power of Action-Based Goals

We all have exciting long-term goals—we want the successful career and to feel great about ourselves—but once we wrap our heads around what it will take for us to reach those long-term goals, we can become demotivated. That makes it even harder for us to take action. You still need those long-term goals, but the trick is to focus on the actions you need to take today, and in the moment, to achieve that goal. Let me share what this action-based goal looks like for me.

I've been going to the gym and working out regularly for over fifteen years, but it was always with the goal of losing fat, building muscle, and becoming a beast in the gym. Those were all outcome-based goals, and even though I got in better shape, I didn't always enjoy working out, and I never quite accomplished those goals I set out to achieve. Recently, I changed tactics and set the simple action-based goal of moving my body every day. That could involve going to the gym, doing yoga, going for a run, or doing workouts at home. I made sure to celebrate myself every time I accomplished that action-based goal, especially when I didn't want to do it. After the first month, I realized that I was working out more often because, once I got moving, I became motivated to continue. A few months later, I was in the best shape of my life. I did that by not thinking about the outcome at all. I just made sure to move my body every day and congratulate myself for showing up.

Even the simple act of taking action can jumpstart the dopamine release process. Remember that motivation follows action, especially when you start to see positive results, so don't wait to feel motivated. For example, when you push yourself to go to the gym and begin working out to achieve a new fitness goal, it might be difficult at first. But putting in the effort and beginning to see results releases dopamine and becomes its own reward. It's motivating. It makes you want to go back. You become motivated through consistency.

This is also the reason why keystone habits are so powerful because when you begin seeing results at the gym, you want more results. You might start going five days a week instead of three, or try to improve your nutrition and sleep to further those fitness goals. Pretty soon, you're hooked on the process. It all goes back to momentum. Once you get rolling, it's easier to keep rolling along. Dopamine can increase your motivation, so you can keep your momentum. That's why action-based goals are so effective.

For the time being, don't worry about the end result. Think about what you want, the actions you need to take, the process that it will require, and then develop a dopamine reward system you can attach to those actions so you can fall in love with the process. It's important that you fall in love with the *process*, not just the end result, because that will keep you moving in a consistent path toward your long-term goals. And you will hit those goals if you're taking the right action. The secret to creating a good action-based goal is to focus on today, and make sure that you act in alignment with the type of person you need to become. That means:

- Attach the reward to the action-based goal of making the calls, not making the sale.

- Attach the reward to the action-based goal of finishing the work-out, not losing weight.

- Attach the reward to the action-based goal of reading five pages, not finishing the book.

- Attach the reward to the action-based goal of eating the healthy meal, not the way you look in the mirror.

- Attach the reward to the action-based goal of practicing for an hour, not winning the championship.

- Attach the reward to the action-based goal of learning one difficult bar of music, not playing the entire piece.

Attaching a dopamine reward to the completion of action-based goals is like a superpower that will make it more likely that you show up every day until you have created a new habit. More important, it puts you in the driver's seat. It puts you in control of when you feel good, but don't get too comfortable. Your brain is smart, and it will adapt. It will recognize the pattern, and once the brain starts to expect dopamine at a certain time or anticipate when it will receive it, that dopamine hit won't have the same impact. When that happens, it might be a little bit harder to continue because you aren't quite as excited as you were the last time. You must switch up the reward system, and every once in a while, skip the reward.

Dopamine is so incredibly powerful, but you don't need to rely on it to do all the work. It's about putting all of these steps of the process together. Understanding why you aren't taking action, implementing the tricks to help you start taking action, and utilizing the science to make it stick create the jet fuel that will propel you to do hard things and reach your goals.

Journal Prompts

- How can you celebrate yourself just for showing up and taking the right action?

- Write down a list of action-based goals that will get you closer to your outcome-based goal that you can then attach a reward system to.

- What will that reward system be for each action or process?

- List some ways that you can naturally increase your dopamine levels throughout the day.

For more journal prompts and video lessons from this book, go to: https://RobDial.com/LevelUp.

Epilogue

I've been in the self-development game for more than fifteen years, and here's the thing: every single person needs to work on themselves, but most just don't realize it. It's not that something is wrong with you. The best way that I've heard it described is to picture yourself walking into an old, abandoned house. You make your way up to a dusty attic that nobody has stepped foot in for decades. In the corner is a mirror covered in dirt and grime. You can barely see your reflection in it, so you try to clean it off, but once you start wiping it down, all of the dirt and dust fly up into your face. To see the clean version of yourself in the mirror, you have to take off a lot of dirt first.

That's what you're doing when you work on yourself. That's self-development. We're all clean mirrors below the surface. That's our true self, but we've developed habits, programs, and systems around who society has told us we're supposed to be and how we're supposed to act. All of that stuff prevents us from achieving our true potential. That's the dirt we're trying to remove, and everybody has it—they just don't know it.

You're here to clean the mirror, and if you've made it this far, you're starting to see the dust and the dirt come off. That dirt is not your true self; there is no reason to judge yourself or place blame.

Just stay focused on the task at hand, which is uncovering your true self under all the dust. If you've read this book, done the work, and still feel discouraged or overwhelmed by all of the aspects of yourself you have to work on, take the time to look back and see how far you've come since you started the book. What have you learned? How have you grown? How much clearer are you about who you are and where you want to go? How much action have you already taken that you wouldn't have taken otherwise? Focus on the wins, and don't allow your brain to dwell on the negative.

The other glaring problem I see when people take on self-development is thinking that the journey has an end, that the mirror will stay clean. As I've learned during my own self-development journey, it is never over. I hear things all the time like "I can't wait until I'm past all of my traumas and don't have to work on myself anymore," but you can't think like that. This work is an ongoing process. Enjoy the journey.

As I said earlier, when you're in a jar, you can't read the label. The goal is to be able to step back and see what's actually happening in your life—recognize the programming, identify where it came from, and be okay with all of the flaws and slow progress. I used to get angry at situations very easily and stay upset for a long time. I could be angry for an entire week, forget about what got me upset, and still feel angry. When I started working on myself, I'd be angry for five days, then three days. Today, I might be upset for only one day. I still get angry—it's an ongoing thing that I work on—but I recognize triggers and am able to step back and calm myself so that I move on more quickly. So when an emotional trigger pops up ten, twenty, or thirty years down the road, you can step back, get yourself out of the jar, identify that trigger, know what you need to work on, and get better for next time.

You may never get to a place where you don't have any baggage or flaws or triggers or where you won't be offended and don't have a temper or show any negative emotion. You may never reach the point where you can remain perfectly calm in the middle of a tornado. That's life, and it's beautiful. Stop trying to control that and learn to enjoy the journey.

I look at personal development as a lifetime journey. You always have room to grow. What's ironic is that coming to terms with that is not overwhelming and daunting; it's actually liberating. It allows you to release that feeling of needing to complete the journey so you can enjoy the process instead. Working through your issues and making improvements will make you proud. You will be able to look back and see how far you've come. And you will realize that in five or ten years, you can do the same thing and look back and be proud of how much progress you have made from this point right now.

I end this book with the six steps of a focused work protocol that you need in order to level up. Whatever your goal, you're going to step out of your comfort zone, face your fear, and combine everything we've learned so far into the following ritual that will help you take action, change your brain, and get it to stick. The six steps are:

1. Focus

2. Work

3. Persist

4. Rest

5. Reward

6. Repeat

What's great about this process is that it can work for so many different tasks. You can do this if you're writing a book, putting together a presentation, trying to study, or just hammering out administrative paperwork. Let's look at each step using the example of learning to play a new piece on the guitar.

1. Focus

Get into the zone just like you would if you had a computer in front of you and were preparing to study or create a presentation. You first want to make sure the conditions are optimal, which means eliminating distractions. Put your phone away and set yourself up in an area where you won't be disturbed.

Once you're set, pick a focal point and stare at something for two minutes that is the same distance away as what you will work on. Try not to blink much. Block out your peripheral vision and try to get into the zone by narrowing your visual field because mental focus follows visual focus. You could stare at the fretboard of the guitar while you warm up your fingers by playing scales to prepare you for when you encounter resistance.

2. Work

Set a timer (not on your phone) for twenty-five minutes and focus on your task, and only that task, for the duration of this first session. Don't try to tackle an entire piece. Start small and focus on the first few bars. Play them over and over until you have mastered those opening notes. Then you can move on to the next part. If that doesn't happen during this first session, that's fine. Just keep practicing until you learn.

3. Persist

Understand that it will take a few minutes for the brain to warm up, and even once it does, you will experience frustration because you will mess up. Your brain is dying for you to go back and play the pieces you already know because it doesn't have to work hard to play them—but don't give in or quit. That agitation is the brain releasing the epinephrine and acetylcholine required to change your brain. The epinephrine creates alertness, while the acetylcholine acts as a highlighter to mark those neurons that will be changed during this process. Every time you mess up, you bring more focus to the task. Your brain won't learn without failing, so you will pick up the new piece much more quickly if you make mistakes than you would if you nailed it on the first try. (And once you do nail it, do it again to be sure.) Remember that making mistakes is important because it's how your brain learns. If you get distracted or your mind wanders, keep pulling yourself back to the task at hand until the timer goes off after the first session.

4. Rest

The first type of rest you want to focus on is a short five-minute break after that first twenty-five-minute session. Don't reach for your phone or do anything stimulating. Go outside and stare at the land-scape if possible. If not, close your eyes and let your mind wander. During this rest period your brain recalibrates, so this is when true learning occurs. This learning will be accelerated when you sleep at night. Make sure you get a good night's sleep.

5. Reward

Don't forget to celebrate yourself. Doing something new is frustrating, and you may not think you're making any progress, but you're trying something outside of your comfort zone that you had been resisting, and that alone is an accomplishment. It doesn't have to be a big celebration, but create some form of dopamine reward system. Something as simple as congratulating yourself out loud or eating a little piece of chocolate after each twenty-five-minute interval will give your brain the boost it needs to keep going. Dopamine is subjective, meaning what releases dopamine for one person doesn't necessarily release it for another, so come up with something you know will motivate you. You want to get excited about the progress that you just made. Even if that progress seems minimal, you still moved the needle, and that's what's important because it will make you more likely to keep showing up.

6. Repeat

After the five-minute break, sit down for another session and repeat this process up to four times. When you're done, you might have made it all the way through the new piece and have made a big improvement. That's great, but don't be surprised if you pick up your guitar tomorrow and can't remember everything. The reason is that your brain changed only chemically. Repetition is required to change your brain structurally and for it to file this action away in its long-term memory. There is no shortcut. It will take practice and repetition, but you will get there in time. Practice enough, and that guitar piece will become another song you can play on autopilot, and that's when you know that you've changed the function of your brain. But you must be consistent.

* * *

Don't forget that focus is a mental muscle, which means that you can make it stronger over time through this process. So even though this six-step protocol will help you learn these skills and get them to stick in the long term, you will also become better at focusing and the protocol itself, which makes this process even more efficient. The trick is to push yourself to focus a little bit longer. Slowly try to expand those twenty-five-minute work sessions up to forty-five minutes. That will enhance the plasticity of that focusing system, and you will experience improvement.

I've watched this happen to many of my clients. At first, they may struggle to focus, but after a month of consistent work, they can't believe how good they get at focusing. The protocol is part of the secret and what helps you prioritize the needle-moving activities so you can cross them off your list every day without fail. Once you've learned how to utilize neuroplasticity and dopamine rewards to make your habits and rituals consistent, you've got all the tools necessary to take

the action required to achieve your goals and reach the next level.
Nothing will stand in your way except for you. You are the CEO of
your own life and the one in control of your own destiny. Go out
and make the best of it!

> You are the CEO of your own life and
> the one in control of your own destiny.
> Go out and make the best of it!

LEVEL UP
FOCUSED WORK PROTOCOL

———————

Rip out this page and put it on your desk, on your computer, or any place where you will see it every day.

1. Focus

Get into the zone.

2. Work

Engage in the task at hand for twenty-five minutes.

3. Persist

Fight through the agitation.

4. Rest

Take a five-minute break.

5. Reward

Celebrate yourself.

6. Repeat

Do it again, and again, and again . . .

Notes

Chapter 1. Fear: None of It Is Real

1. E. J. Gibson and R. D. Walk, "The Visual Cliff," *Scientific American* 202, no. 4 (1960): 64–71.
2. I. M. Knudson and J. R. Melcher, "Elevated Acoustic Startle Responses in Humans: Relationship to Reduced Loudness Discomfort Level, but Not Self-Report of Hyperacusis," *Journal of the Association for Research Otolaryngology* 17, no. 3 (2016): 223–35, doi: 10.1007/s10162-016-0555-y.
3. Karl Albrecht, "The (Only) 5 Fears We All Share," *Psychology Today*, March 22, 2012, https://www.psychologytoday.com/us/blog /brainsnacks/201203/the-only-5-fears-we-all-share.
4. Don Joseph Goewey, "85 Percent of What We Worry About Never Happens," *HuffPost*, last updated December 6, 2017, https://www.huffpost .com/entry/85-of-what-we-worry-about_b_8028368.
5. Bart Massi, Christopher H. Donahue, and Daeyeol Lee, "Volatility Facilitates Value Updating in the Prefrontal Cortex," *Neuron* 99, no. 3 (2018): 598–608, https://doi.org/10.1016/j.neuron.2018.06.033.

Chapter 2. Identity: You Aren't the Person You Think You Are

1. "What Is Personality?," OpenEd CUNY, accessed April 10, 2023, https:// opened.cuny.edu/courseware/lesson/66/student/.
2. Maxwell Maltz, quoted on https://www.whatshouldireadnext.com/quotes /maxwell-maltz-a-human-being-always-acts.
3. Emma Young, "Lifting the Lid on the Unconscious," NewScientist, July 25, 2018, https://www.newscientist.com/article/mg23931880-400 -lifting-the-lid-on-the-unconscious/.

4. "Kelley and Conner's Emotional Cycle of Change," *Mind Tools*, accessed April 10, 2023, https://www.mindtools.com/apjsz96/kelley-and-conners-emotional-cycle-of-change.
5. "Why Do Lottery Winners Go Broke?," Money Marshmallow, January 2, 2023, https://moneymarshmallow.com/why-do-lottery-winners-go-broke/.
6. A. Hatzigeorgiadis, N. Zourbanos, E. Galanis, and Y. Theodorakis, "Self-Talk and Sports Performance: A Meta-Analysis," *Perspectives on Psychological Science* 6, no. 4 (2011): 348–56, https://doi.org/10.1177/1745691611413136.

Chapter 3. Purpose: What Do You Want?

1. Gail Matthews, "Goals Research Summary," https://www.dominican.edu/sites/default/files/2020-02/gailmatthews-harvard-goals-researchsummary.pdf.

Chapter 4. Visualization: The Bridge to Action

1. "Understanding Unconscious Bias," *Short Wave*, July 15, 2020, https://www.npr.org/transcripts/891140598.
2. T. Blankert and M. R. Hamstra, "Imagining Success: Multiple Achievement Goals and the Effectiveness of Imagery," *Basic and Applied Social Psychology* 39, no. 1 (2017): 60–67, doi: 10.1080/01973533.2016.1255947.

Chapter 6. Distraction: The Enemy of Action

1. Kirsten Weir, "Nurtured by Nature," *Monitor on Psychology* 51, no. 3 (April 1, 2020): 50, https://www.apa.org/monitor/2020/04/nurtured-nature.
2. T. D. Wilson, D. A. Reinhard, E. C. Westgate, D. T. Gilbert, N. Ellerbeck, C. Hahn, C. L. Brown, and A. Shaked, "Just Think: The Challenges of the Disengaged Mind," *Science* 345, no. 6192 (2014): 75–77, doi: 10.1126/science.1250830.
3. Ron Marshall, "How Many Ads Do You See in One Day?," Red Crow Marketing Inc., September 10, 2015, https://www.redcrowmarketing.com/2015/09/10/many-ads-see-one-day/.
4. Trevor Wheelwright, "2022 Cell Phone Usage Statistics: How Obsessed Are We?," Reviews.org, January 24, 2022, https://www.reviews.org/mobile/cell-phone-addiction/.
5. P. Lorenz-Spreen, B. M. Mønsted, P. Hövel, and S. Lehmann, "Accelerating Dynamics of Collective Attention," *Nature Communications* 10, no. 1759 (2019), https://doi.org/10.1038/s41467-019-09311-w; Sandee LaMotte, "Your Attention Span Is Shrinking, Studies Say. Here's How to Stay

Focused," CNN Health, January 22, 2023, https://www.cnn.com /2023/01/11/health/short-attention-span-wellness/index.html; Kevin McSpadden, "You Now Have a Shorter Attention Span than a Goldfish," *TIME*, May 14, 2015, https://time.com/3858309/attention-spans -goldfish/.

6. William Parker, "During Quarantine: How Much Netflix Did We Watch? Data + Content Streaming Stats," HotDog.com, last updated August 25, 2022, https://hotdog.com/tv/stream/netflix/during-quarantine/.

7. Matt Gonzales, "How Long Does Alcohol Stay in Your System (Blood, Urine and Saliva)?," DrugRehab.com, April 20, 2020, https://www.drugrehab.com /addiction/alcohol/how-long-does-alcohol-stay-in-your-system/.

Chapter 7. One Step at a Time: How to Get It All Done

1. Conor J. Wild, Emily S. Nichols, Michael E. Battista, Bobby Stojanoski, and Adrian M. Owen, "Dissociable Effects of Self-Reported Daily Sleep Duration on High-Level Cognitive Abilities," *Sleep* 41, no. 12 (2018), https://doi.org/10.1093/sleep/zsy182.

2. Mariana G. Figueiro, Bryan Steverson, Judith Heerwagen, Kevin Kampschroer, Claudia M. Hunter, Kassandra Gonzales, Barbara Plitnick, and Mark S. Rea, "The Impact of Daytime Light Exposures on Sleep and Mood in Office Workers," *Sleep Health* 3, no. 3 (2017): 204–15.

3. See, for instance, K. Choi, C. Shin, T. Kim, H. J. Chung, and H.-J. Suk, "Awakening Effects of Blue-Enriched Morning Light Exposure on University Students' Physiological and Subjective Responses," *Scientific Reports* 9, no. 345 (2019), https://doi.org/10.1038/s41598-018-36791-5; and A. U. Viola, L. M. James, L. J. M. Schlangen, and D.-J. Dijk, "Blue-Enriched White Light in the Workplace Improves Self-Reported Alertness, Performance and Sleep Quality," *Scandinavian Journal of Work, Environment & Health* 34, no. 4 (2008): 297–306.

4. K. R. Westerterp, "Diet Induced Thermogenesis," *Nutrition & Metabolism* 1, no. 5 (2004), https://doi.org/10.1186/1743-7075-1-5.

5. Jip Gudden, Alejandro Arias Vasquez, and Mirjam Bloemendaal, "The Effects of Intermittent Fasting on Brain and Cognitive Function," *Nutrients* 13, no. 9 (September 2021): 3166, https://www.ncbi.nlm.nih.gov/pmc /articles/PMC8470960/.

6. For instance, see Molly Hodges, "The Effects of Dehydration on Cognitive Functioning, Mood, and Physical Performance," *Corinthian* 13, no. 2 (2012), https://kb.gcsu.edu/thecorinthian/vol13/iss1/2.

7. Jennifer B. Dowd, Nalini Ranjit, D. Phuong Do, Elizabeth A. Young, James S. House, and George Kaplan, "Education and Levels of Salivary

Cortisol over the Day in US Adults," *Annals of Behavioral Medicine* 41, no. 1 (February 2011): 13–20, doi: 10.1007/s12160-010-9224-2.

8. A. Gawron-Gzella, J. Chanaj-Kaczmarek, and J. Cielecka-Piontek, "Yerba Mate: A Long but Current History," *Nutrients* 13, no. 11 (2021): 3706, doi: 10.3390/nu13113706; A. Gambero and M. L. Ribeiro, "The Positive Effects of Yerba Maté (*Ilex paraguariensis*) in Obesity," *Nutrients* 7, no. 2 (2015): 730–50, doi: 10.3390/nu7020730.

Chapter 8. Focus: The Secret to Productivity

1. "Attention," *New World Encyclopedia*, accessed April 10, 2023, https://www.newworldencyclopedia.org/entry/Attention.

2. L. Zylowska, D. L. Ackerman, M. H. Yang, J. L. Futrell, N. L. Horton, T. S. Hale, C. Pataki, and S. L. Smalley, "Mindfulness Meditation Training in Adults and Adolescents with ADHD: A Feasibility Study," *Journal of Attention Disorders* 11, no. 6 (2008): 737–46, https://doi.org/10.1177/1087054707308502.

3. Melanie Curtin, "In an Eight-Hour Day, the Average Worker Is Productive for This Many Hours," *Inc.*, July 21, 2016, https://www.inc.com/melanie-curtin/in-an-8-hour-day-the-average-worker-is-productive-for-this-many-hours.html.

4. Bret Stetka, "Our Brain Uses a Not-So-Instant Replay to Make Decisions," *Scientific American*, June 27, 2019, https://www.scientificamerican.com/article/our-brain-uses-a-not-so-instant-replay-to-make-decisions/.

5. Sophie Leroy, "Why Is It So Hard to Do My Work? The Challenge of Attention Residue When Switching Between Work Tasks," *Organizational Behavior and Human Decision Processes* 109, no. 2 (2009): 168–81, https://doi.org/10.1016/j.obhdp.2009.04.002; Kevin P. Madore and Anthony D. Wagner, "Multicosts of Multitasking," *Cerebrum*, April 1, 2019, https://www.ncbi.nlm.nih.gov/pmc/articles/PMC7075496/.

6. Paul Atchley, "You Can't Multitask, So Stop Trying," *Harvard Business Review*, December 21, 2010, https://hbr.org/2010/12/you-cant-multi-task-so-stop-tr.

7. Cal Newport, *Deep Work: Rules for Focused Success in a Distracted World* (New York: Grand Central, 2016).

8. "Episode 57: Optimizing Workspace for Productivity, Focus, & Creativity," *Huberman Lab*, January 31, 2022, https://podcastnotes.org/huberman-lab/episode-57-optimizing-workspace-for-productivity-focus-creativity-huberman-lab/.

9. "Episode 57: Optimizing Workspace for Productivity, Focus, & Creativity," *Huberman Lab*.

10. "Blue Light May Fight Fatigue Around the Clock," ScienceDaily, February 3, 2014, https://www.sciencedaily.com/releases/2014/02/140203191841.htm.

11. R. Hardeland, "Melatonin, Hormone of Darkness and More: Occurrence, Control Mechanisms, Actions and Bioactive Metabolites," *Cellular and Molecular Life Sciences* 65, no. 13 (2008): 2001–18, doi: 10.1007/s00018-008-8001-x.

12. S. Basu and B. Banerjee, "Potential of Binaural Beats Intervention for Improving Memory and Attention: Insights from Meta-Analysis and Systematic Review," *Psychological Research*, July 16, 2022, online ahead of print, doi: 10.1007/s00426-022-01706-7.

13. Nicole Baum and Jasleen Chaddha, "The Impact of Auditory White Noise on Cognitive Performance," *Journal of Science and Medicine* 3, special issue, (2021): 1–15, https://doi.org/10.37714/josam.v3i0.82.

14. Jessica Stillman, "How Exercise Makes You Smarter, Happier, and Less Stressed," *Inc.*, February 17, 2016, https://www.inc.com/jessica-stillman/how-to-use-exercise-to-optimize-your-brain.html.

15. T. M. Altenburg, M. J. Chinapaw, and A. S. Singh, "Effects of One Versus Two Bouts of Moderate Intensity Physical Activity on Selective Attention During a School Morning in Dutch Primary Schoolchildren: A Randomized Controlled Trial," *Journal of Science and Medicine in Sport* 19, no. 10 (2016): 820–24, doi: 10.1016/j.jsams.2015.12.003.

16. A. Mooventhan and L. Nivethitha, "Scientific Evidence-Based Effects of Hydrotherapy on Various Systems of the Body," *North American Journal of Medicine and Science* 6, no. 5 (2014): 199–209, doi: 10.4103/1947-2714.132935.

Chapter 9. Consistency: How to Show Up Every Day

1. Jeff Haden, "Want to Improve Your Performance? Science Says Harness the Power of Rituals," *Inc.*, September 21, 2021, https://www.inc.com/jeff-haden/how-to-improve-performance-productivity-results-rituals-routines-processes-rafael-nadal.html.

2. Darren Hardy, *The Compound Effect: Jumpstart Your Income, Your Life, Your Success* (New York: Vanguard, 2012), 42.

Chapter 10. Habits: How to Make Taking Action Effortless

1. Steve Bradt, "Wandering Mind Not a Happy Mind," *Harvard Gazette*, November 11, 2010, https://news.harvard.edu/gazette/story/2010/11/wandering-mind-not-a-happy-mind/.

2. "How Your Brain Makes and Uses Energy," Queensland Brain Institute, University of Queensland, https://qbi.uq.edu.au/brain/nature-discovery/how-your-brain-makes-and-uses-energy.

3. "What Is Emotional Eating?," Cleveland Clinic, November 12, 2021, https://health.clevelandclinic.org/emotional-eating/.

4. Scott Frothingham, "How Long Does It Take for a New Behavior to Become Automatic?," Healthline, October 24, 2019, https://www.healthline.com/health/how-long-does-it-take-to-form-a-habit.

Chapter 11. Neuroplasticity: The Science of Changing Your Brain

1. Ferris Jabr, "Cache Cab: Taxi Drivers' Brains Grow to Navigate London's Streets," *Scientific American*, December 8, 2011, https://www.scientificamerican.com/article/london-taxi-memory/.

2. Nathan Collins, "Pathways: From the Eye to the Brain," *Stanford Medicine Magazine*, August 21, 2017, https://stanmed.stanford.edu/carla-shatz-vision-brain/.

3. L. M. Shin, S. L. Rauch, and R. K. Pitman, "Amygdala, Medial Prefrontal Cortex, and Hippocampal Function in PTSD," *Annals of the New York Academy of Sciences* 1071 (2006): 67–79, doi: 10.1196/annals.1364.007.

4. K. Susuki, "Myelin: A Specialized Membrane for Cell Communication," *Nature Education* 3, no. 9 (2010): 59.

5. Sandra Ackerman, "From Chemistry to Circuitry," in *Discovering the Brain* (Washington, DC: National Academies Press, 1992).

6. I. G. Meister, T. Krings, H. Foltys, B. Boroojerdi, M. Müller, R. Töpper, and A. Thron, "Playing Piano in the Mind: An fMRI Study on Music Imagery and Performance in Pianists," *Cognitive Brain Research* 19, no. 3 (2004): 219–28, https://doi.org/10.1016/j.cogbrainres.2003.12.005.

7. Ian Sample, "Scientists Shed Light on Creativity by Studying Pianists' Brain Activity," *The Guardian*, November 12, 2013, https://www.theguardian.com/science/2013/nov/12/scientists-creativity-pianists-brain-activity.

8. Christopher N. Cascio, Matthew Brook O'Donnell, Francis J. Tinney, Matthew D. Lieberman, Shelley E. Taylor, Victor J. Strecher, and Emily B. Falk, "Self-Affirmation Activates Brain Systems Associated with Self-Related Processing and Reward and Is Reinforced by Future Orientation," *Social Cognitive and Affective Neuroscience* 11, no. 4 (April 2016): 621–29, doi: 10.1093/scan/nsv136.

9. J. David Creswell, William T. Welch, Shelley E. Taylor, David K. Sherman, Tara L. Gruenewald, and Traci Mann, "Affirmation of Personal Values

Buffers Neuroendocrine and Psychological Stress Responses," *Psychological Science* 16, no. 11 (November 2005): 846–51.

10. Alan Rozanski, Chirag Bavishi, Laura D. Kubzansky, and Randy Cohen, "Association of Optimism with Cardiovascular Events and All-Cause Mortality: A Systematic Review and Meta-Analysis," *JAMA Network Open* 2, no. 9 (September 27, 2019): e1912200, doi: 10.1001/jamanetworkopen .2019.12200.

11. S. Pangambam, "Transcript: After Watching This, Your Brain Will Not Be the Same by Lara Boyd," Singju Post, June 24, 2016, https://singjupost.com /transcript-after-watching-this-your-brain-will-not-be-the-same-by-lara -boyd/?singlepage=1.

12. S. Diekelmann, I. Wilhelm, and J. Born, "The Whats and Whens of Sleep-Dependent Memory Consolidation," *Sleep Medicine Reviews* 13, no. 5 (2009): 309–21.

13. H. Freyja Ólafsdóttir, Daniel Bush, and Caswell Barry, "The Role of Hippocampal Replay in Memory and Planning," *Current Biology* 28, no. 1 (2018): R37–R50, https://doi.org/10.1016/j.cub.2017.10.073.

Chapter 12. Creating a Dopamine Reward System: Falling in Love with the Process

1. For instance, J. Yim, "Therapeutic Benefits of Laughter in Mental Health: A Theoretical Review," *Tohoku Journal of Experimental Medicine* 239, no. 3 (2016): 243–49.

2. "Episode 39: Controlling Your Dopamine for Motivation, Focus & Satisfaction," *Huberman Lab*, September 29, 2021, https://podcastnotes .org/huberman-lab/episode-39-controlling-your-dopamine-for-motivation -focus-satisfaction-huberman-lab/.